REMADE Series

RENEWED

Renewed: A 6-Week Personal or Small Group Study
Copyright ©2023 Michelle Rayburn
ISBN: 978-1-954576-01-8

Published by Faith Creativity Life Books
fclbooks.com

Unless otherwise indicated, all Scripture quotations are taken from the *Holy Bible*, New Living Translation, copyright © 1996, 2004, 2015 by Tyndale House Foundation. Used by permission of Tyndale House Publishers, Inc., Carol Stream, Illinois 60188. All rights reserved.

Scriptures marked AMP are from the Amplified® Bible, Copyright © 2015 by The Lockman Foundation. Used by permission. lockman.org

Edited by Robyn Mulder – robynmulder.com
Cover and typesetting by Michelle Rayburn – missionandmedia.com
Cover image, royalty-free, Storyblocks – storyblocks.com

Books in the REMADE series:

Renewed (2023)

Refreshed (2023)

Restored (2024)

Refined (2024)

REMADE Series

RENEWED

A 6-Week Personal
or Small Group Study

Michelle
Rayburn

BOOKS

Christine Zoe,

you truly live the meaning of your names:
"follower of Christ" and "life."
I'm inspired by your story of renewal
and forever grateful for four decades of
support and encouragement.

Contents

Welcome

OVER THE COMING WEEKS, WE WILL STUDY what it means to be renewed. To be changed in such a way that we see how our experiences—good or bad—fit together into a work of art. It may not make sense at first, but it's beautiful, just the same.

If you're a fan of television shows featuring before-and-after makeovers, then you already appreciate the wonder of something remade.

If you don't enjoy DIY projects, power tools, or the glory of getting globs of paint in your hair, you've probably rolled your eyes and humored a fanatic friend at least once. And if envisioning the possibilities in a piece of thrift-sale junk is as confusing as deciphering hieroglyphics, I have a feeling you've at least dropped your jaw for a finished transformation when the artist revealed the *after* version.

We love amazing results! But before we get to the outcome, we sift through the junk, looking for something to repurpose. So, let's start there. This is your opportunity to explore the amazing way God transforms what might seem to be hopeless causes into masterpieces—scars and all.

I'm excited for you to explore what an encounter with Jesus did for Saul and the radical way this transformed him! I encourage you to be vulnerable with your responses and tender with others as they share. This is a safe space to be authentic.

WHAT TO EXPECT

I'VE SELECTED THE NEW LIVING TRANSLATION (NLT) for any Bible passages printed in this study. However, you're always welcome to use your favorite translation. I chose the NLT because it's worded in such a way that people from all backgrounds can understand. If you didn't grow up in church, you might see Scripture as difficult to understand. Or perhaps you memorized verses from a Bible version that used Old English, and it's nostalgic to you. We can celebrate our wide-ranging styles and understanding.

There is nothing wrong with those translations. But I've found that teaching from the NLT text helps many people feel more comfortable discussing and applying biblical principles to life. Whether you've been studying the Bible for years or recently started, you can explore Scripture and discover something that speaks to your situation. Take as long as you need to study and process the content in each chapter.

LEADERS

If you're doing this as a group, you probably have someone designated as a leader. That's great! We all need someone to keep us on task. You might wonder why this study doesn't include a leader guide. Great question.

Think of your leader as a facilitator. Her role is to keep the discussion moving and watch for opportunities to draw everyone into the conversation. She's the sister who wants to ensure each person feels loved, valued, and heard.

Here's what she does not need to do: spend hours prepping, study the Hebrew and Greek and a stack of commentaries, and come to the group ready to teach. *Whew!* I heard someone breathe a sigh of relief there.

I've found that when we all come to the topic prepared to share our hearts rather than teach a lesson, there is a sweet, mutual blessing that comes from thinking together. Asking the questions and reflecting out loud. Being real and not needing to know all the things.

This study is a guide for you. I don't know *all* the things either. God's beautiful and powerful Word has an endless supply of wisdom to study and apply. Do it together. Explore it *with* each other. And take the pressure off someone to lead.

Maybe you'll read that and raise your hand to be the next facilitator.

GROUPS AND INDIVIDUALS

If your group has more than eight participants, I encourage you to do the story part together and then cluster into smaller groups for discussion and study.

This will also provide a better space for each person to contribute to the discussion. The shy or introverted ones have something to say—probably profound and thoughtful—if you make space for conversation.

This study can also be done online through video chat. There is no video component to worry about coordinating. With a workbook, a Bible, and a device with a camera, anyone can join in for discussion.

If you're doing the study on your own, you might consider having a friend do it simultaneously. You could have a weekly chat to share prayer needs with one another and talk about what you're applying that week to your life. Or you could enlist a few friends and have a Facebook group with weekly posts, an Instagram group chat, or a Discord or Slack discussion.*

Whether you meet in a coffee shop, the church fellowship hall, your living room, or a virtual space, the goal is the same: growing connections with one another around the Word of God.

FORMAT

IN THIS QUICK RUN-THROUGH OF THE WEEKLY format, I'll give you some ideas for ways you can use the material. You never have to do *all* of it. If you have less than ninety minutes each week for a group meeting, or if you need extra social time when you gather, you might spread out the six lessons over twelve weeks.

There is no right way to do it. I know there is at least one perfectionist out there who needs that permission to go off script and feel the freedom of seeing where the road leads. You're welcome.

First Thoughts
This is a time of reflection before the study begins. It's solo work for you to do as you tune out distractions and prepare your mind and heart for what God might do. Allow five to ten minutes to forget the dishes you left in the sink and the errand list calling to you. Silence your smartphone and pause.

Story
This is your warmup. I'll start you off with a short personal story to introduce the chapter. If you're in a group, you could have someone read this aloud, have everyone read it ahead of time, or take turns reading the section. It's also my way of saying, "If we're all going to be vulnerable here, I'll go first."

Prayer
Have someone read it aloud to prepare your hearts for study. Or pray in your own words! It's a starting point.

Explore the Word
This section gets to the heart of the study. Many of the Bible passages will be printed in the text. This will help if you all have different translations. You can read together but use your Bible for a parallel study with footnotes and more.

---

* See Discord.com or Slack.com.

There are additional notes, Bible verses, and commentary in the sidebars. These are for further study if you'd like to explore more, go deeper, take a detour, or spread the lesson over more than one week—any way you'd like to use them.

Again, this is designed for you to read, study, and discuss together without anyone needing to teach.

Prayer Journal

The prayer journal can be used on your own, in the group, or both. I know how groups can get off track when it comes to prayer time. Our intentions are pure. They really are! But sometimes one person talks a lot. And someone else doesn't know how to put her needs into words. Or someone else needs a moment to gather her thoughts and process.

One way to make your prayer time more intimate is to take a moment to write in the prayer journal. Then, divide into groups of two to three people to share one thing you wrote there. You can pray specifically over these praises or requests together and even plan to check in once during the week with the people in your prayer cluster—perhaps by text, phone call, or email.

Look back each week and note where you saw God in action on the things you included in your prayers.

Micro Studies

There are five devotional studies for you to do on your own during the week. Or, if you're doing this book solo, you might want to complete the main study one week and the micro studies the next and stretch it out over twelve weeks.

The micro studies are geared toward personal application of the main Bible study. Each one has a passage to read, a verse to write out, an application question, and a place for you to write a prayer that day.

Hope in Action

When faith, creativity, and everyday life intersect, it's beautiful! Not everyone is crafty, so I promise you'll find a variety of action steps here that connect the weekly topic with an idea you can carry out in a practical way. Some are artsy, but they're mostly geared toward loving and encouraging others.

Before you begin, I'd like to pray for you:

Heavenly Father, I pray on behalf of the woman holding this book. Whether she's on her own or with friends, you are here with her. As she opens your Word and opens her heart, I ask that you renew her in a way only you can. Where tender feelings ache or painful memories arise, be the balm that soothes wounds and heals raw emotions. In hardened or calloused places, gently soften and prepare for renewal. As your work begins, make your presence evident in this sweet sister's life and stir up a sense of hope leading to a joyful celebration of your power over bondage. Thank you for the freedom you bring when we are remade by grace and shaped by your love. Amen.

WEEK ONE
REDEEM

But he was pierced for our rebellion, crushed for our sins. He was beaten so we could be whole. He was whipped so we could be healed. —Isaiah 53:5

First Thoughts

TAKE A FEW MOMENTS TO LINGER ON these questions before we get started. It's okay if the thoughts come slow and muddled. Messy is perfectly acceptable here. Scars and flaws are welcome. God is the master of remaking broken into beautiful.

- Right now, I would love to find joy in the middle of _____ _____.

- In my life, it would be a miracle if _____ _____.

- When I consider my current circumstances, I don't see the purpose for _____.

- I felt broken, worthless, unimportant, or tossed aside when _____. That also made me think _____ _____.

STORY

I'M OBSESSED WITH WORDS THAT BEGIN WITH "re." Welcome to the fascination with words that hold so much promise. Seriously! See if you can stop yourself from thinking of ten words that begin with that little prefix.

Each week, we will focus on a word that begins with "re" that relates—there's another *re* word!—to becoming more like Jesus. We will talk about what it means to be broken and restored and made new—what it means to discover hope where there appears to be no hope. It's about do-overs and fresh starts. About discovering beauty in the trashy stuff of life.

Let's step into a fixer-upper sort of mindset and think about finding treasures in garage sale and flea market junk. Not everyone loves to sort through a pile of someone else's castoffs on a search for treasure, I know. I'm weird like that. But even if you don't love thrift-sale shopping, it's likely you can appreciate that it's an art.

If you've been to a thrift sale or hosted one, you may have asked or heard, "Does this work?" Most of us don't want to buy something broken, but for the trash-to-treasure fan, even broken things have potential. In their hands, a worn-out typewriter becomes a piece of art. A once-electric teapot becomes a container for flowers—no cord needed. An inoperative camera becomes a conversation piece in a vignette. A malfunctioning lamp becomes a candle sconce. Unlike others, the trash-to-treasure fan sees value in the damaged, wrecked, and discarded.

We live in a world where we throw away broken things. If it's no longer needed, we get rid of it. If an item is damaged, beat up, or flawed, we toss it in the trash.

Have you noticed we sometimes do this with people too? A friend speaks the truth, but it hurts our feelings, and we toss the friendship away. We're not sure how to connect with somebody who is a little rough around the edges, so we pretend not to notice their needs. We see a friend heading down a path of wrong decisions, and we turn our back and tell stories about her when we gather for coffee with our other friends. If you've been tossed aside for your broken-ness, you understand the hurt.

There are broken people all around us. Broken hearts, broken relationships, broken trust, broken faith, broken dreams, and broken lives. Perhaps you feel it. The damage has seeped into your core and chipped at your worth.

Our brokenness becomes bondage when we don't see any hope. However, it doesn't have to equal hopelessness. The scars that accompany us everywhere we go don't have to be evidence of hurting but of healing. When we understand that Jesus came for broken people and came to set us free from our ugly past, then we begin to experience hope. We find joy. And we discover beauty in the mess.

Before we jump into the study today, I want you to hear this.

You are loved. I'm glad you're here. No matter what your past contains or what mistakes you've made, you matter, you are important, and you are loved.

If that doesn't resonate or sink in just yet, stick around. As we study Scripture, I hope it will become so evident that God melts away any resistance with his tender grace.

PRAYER

GOD, WE THANK YOU FOR THE INCREDIBLE gift of your Son, who was broken so we might experience freedom. Thank you, Jesus, for taking upon yourself the penalty we deserved. I pray that we might experience the joy of being remade for your glory. We ask specifically for the healing of wounds that keep us from living in the victory you died to give us. We want to be alive in you! Amen.

EXPLORE THE WORD

IN LUKE 4, WE READ OF A time when Jesus was in his hometown of Nazareth, and he went to the synagogue on the Sabbath and stood up to read from the Scriptures.

> Then Jesus returned to Galilee, filled with the Holy
> Spirit's power. Reports about him spread quickly
> through the whole region. He taught regularly in their

synagogues and was praised by everyone. When he came to the village of Nazareth, his boyhood home, he went as usual to the synagogue on the Sabbath and stood up to read the Scriptures. The scroll of Isaiah the prophet was handed to him. He unrolled the scroll and found the place where this was written:

"The Spirit of the Lord is upon me, for he has anointed me to bring Good News to the poor. He has sent me to proclaim that captives will be released, that the blind will see, that the oppressed will be set free, and that the time of the Lord's favor has come."

He rolled up the scroll, handed it back to the attendant, and sat down. All eyes in the synagogue looked at him intently. Then he began to speak to them. "The Scripture you've just heard has been fulfilled this very day!"

Everyone spoke well of him and was amazed by the gracious words that came from his lips. "How can this be?" they asked. "Isn't this Joseph's son?" (Luke 4:14–22)

Perhaps, like me, you missed the little detail that Jesus didn't only preach on hillsides in front of crowds of 5000 people who forgot to pack a lunch. He also taught in the synagogue, the Jewish meeting place. This is in his boyhood hometown

After the liturgical services at the synagogue, the "minister" took a scroll of the law from the ark of the covenant and then called on someone to read. Doing further study, I learned: "On the Sabbaths, at least seven persons were called on successively to read portions of the law, none of them consisting of less than three verses. After the law followed a section from the prophets, which was succeeded immediately by a discourse. It was this section which Jesus read and expounded."[*]

Jesus read from the book of Isaiah. But he didn't only read. Jesus rolled up the scroll and sat down to speak about the passage.

"The Scripture you've just heard has been fulfilled this very day!"

> I always like to know the rest of the story, so let's address the question this raises: From where did Jesus return?
>
> Answer: He had just been in the wilderness, where Satan tempted him. Jesus didn't return depleted from being tempted. He returned filled with the power of the Holy Spirit.

Synagogue
(*synagōgē*). A place for assembly and worship that developed in Jewish communities throughout the Mediterranean in the late centuries BC.[**] This is not to be confused with the temple in Jerusalem. Synagogues were in regional communities.

---

[*] Marvin Richardson Vincent, *Word Studies in the New Testament*, vol. 1 (New York: Charles Scribner's Sons, 1887), 290.

[**] Matthew E. Gordley, "Synagogue," in *The Lexham Bible Dictionary*, ed. John D. Barry et al. (Bellingham, WA: Lexham Press, 2016).

Essentially, he said, "That's me!" Mic drop.

What would you have thought if you had been in the crowd?

Would you have believed Jesus's claim?

All eyes looked at him intently. I can imagine their furrowed brows. A slight head tilt before turning to a neighbor and saying, "Isn't this Joseph's son?" They spoke well of him, it says, and were amazed by the gracious words he spoke. But it didn't last long.

Spoiler alert: they didn't like what he said after that and mobbed him, forcing Jesus to the edge of a cliff they intended to push him over. But let's come back to what he read. Part of it came from this passage:

> The Spirit of the Sovereign LORD is upon me, for the LORD has anointed me to bring good news to the poor. He has sent me to comfort the brokenhearted and to proclaim that captives will be released and prisoners will be freed.
>
> He has sent me to tell those who mourn that the time of the Lord's favor has come, and with it, the day of God's anger against their enemies. To all who mourn in Israel, he will give a crown of beauty for ashes, a joyous blessing instead of mourning, festive praise instead of despair. In their righteousness, they will be like great oaks that the LORD has planted for his own glory. (Isaiah 61:1–3)

To all who mourn in Israel, he will give a crown of beauty for ashes, a joyous blessing instead of mourning, festive praise instead of despair.
—Isaiah 61:3

At that time, wearing sackcloth and covering yourself with ashes could be a sign of mourning, a euphemism showing the frailty of human life. It could also be an expression of remorse.* Sackcloth is a rough fabric similar to burlap, and it was used to make sacks. (Sounds logical, right?) Smearing ashes on yourself and wearing itchy, irritating cloth was an outward sign of what was going on inside.

While I've never owned a burlap dress, I've definitely shown what was going on inside when I've sported a messy ponytail, ragged sweatpants, and a stained sweatshirt on days when fun was swallowed up by function. Can I get a witness?

But there have been days when discouragement, sadness, and frustration hid neatly behind a coordinated outfit, lip gloss and eye shadow, and hair that had been washed and styled instead of dry-shampooed for a week.

However you style it, sadness is a prison for the soul.

When have you been so sad that you've "worn" it on the outside?

I've noticed that this same burlap fabric appears in the decorations at so many modern weddings! Wouldn't that be a shock for someone from biblical times to see? The same material once used for horribly uncomfortable mourning clothes is now used in ribbons and backdrops, wrapped around mason jars, and draped over tables.

The prophet Isaiah proclaimed that his ministry would restore God's people, and then Jesus proclaimed the same mission for his ministry. He came to replace his people's mourning with joy—their filthy ashes would be replaced with a crown of beauty.

Let's consider how long the Jews waited for deliverance. Generation after generation, parents told their children and grandchildren that a Savior, the Messiah, was coming. The coming of the Messiah is a prominent theme in the book of Isaiah.

The "time of the Lord's favor" referred to the Year of Jubilee (explained in Leviticus 25:8–55), a time when slaves were set free and debts canceled. The Year of Jubilee is a metaphor for salvation.

---

* Douglas Estes, "Ashes," in *The Lexham Bible Dictionary*, ed. John D. Barry et al. (Bellingham, WA: Lexham Press, 2016).

How do you think the people felt when they heard Jesus talk about comforting the brokenhearted and setting people free?

Look at these phrases: good news to the poor, captives released, blind will see, oppressed set free, the Lord's favor has come. Is it any wonder that Jesus's hometown friends and relatives wanted to be first in line to receive God's blessings? Of course, they didn't want Jesus to take his miracles anywhere else. Especially not to unclean and lowly outsiders.

Why do you think the people missed their *spiritual* poverty, thinking more of the physical or material blessings Jesus could presumably offer?

Let's read Isaiah 53. As you read, look for Jesus's story in this passage. Highlight or underline anything that points to Jesus.

> [1] Who has believed our message?
>   To whom has the Lord revealed his powerful arm?
> [2] My servant grew up in the Lord's presence like a tender green shoot,
>   like a root in dry ground.
> There was nothing beautiful or majestic about his appearance,
>   nothing to attract us to him.
> [3] He was despised and rejected—
>   a man of sorrows, acquainted with deepest grief.
> We turned our backs on him and looked the other way.

He was despised, and we did not care.
⁴ Yet it was our weaknesses he carried;
    it was our sorrows that weighed him down.
And we thought his troubles were a punishment from God,
    a punishment for his own sins!
⁵ But he was pierced for our rebellion,
    crushed for our sins.
He was beaten so we could be whole.
    He was whipped so we could be healed.
⁶ All of us, like sheep, have strayed away.
    We have left God's paths to follow our own.
Yet the Lord laid on him
    the sins of us all.
⁷ He was oppressed and treated harshly,
    yet he never said a word.
He was led like a lamb to the slaughter.
    And as a sheep is silent before the shearers,
    he did not open his mouth.
⁸ Unjustly condemned,
    he was led away.
No one cared that he died without descendants,
    that his life was cut short in midstream.
But he was struck down
    for the rebellion of my people.
⁹ He had done no wrong
    and had never deceived anyone.
But he was buried like a criminal;
    he was put in a rich man's grave.
¹⁰ But it was the Lord's good plan to crush him
    and cause him grief.
Yet when his life is made an offering for sin,
    he will have many descendants.
He will enjoy a long life,
    and the Lord's good plan will prosper in his hands.
¹¹ When he sees all that is accomplished by his anguish,
    he will be satisfied.

> All of us, like sheep, have strayed away. We have left God's paths to follow our own. Yet the Lord laid on him the sins of us all.

And because of his experience,
> my righteous servant will make it possible
for many to be counted righteous,
> for he will bear all their sins.
[12] I will give him the honors of a victorious soldier,
> because he exposed himself to death.
He was counted among the rebels.
> He bore the sins of many and interceded for rebels.

Notice that the pain, the suffering, and the ugliness alluded to here is about what Jesus was going to do. He was going to purchase our freedom from the bondage of sin. He was called a man of sorrows who knew the deepest of grief (verse 3), and yet, the next verse tells us he carried our own sorrows on himself. On the outside, it looks as if Jesus would carry his own punishment, but then we see that it was *ours*.

Pause to think about that for a moment. It's heavy.

Make a list from that passage of all the ways he suffered:

In verses 5–6, we learn that he endured it all for us. *We* are the ones who wandered away from God like disobedient sheep, but *he* is the one who paid for it.

Look at verse 10 for the heart of the message. God planned for this to happen to Jesus. This is deep and difficult to understand. We might wonder how it can be God's will that someone would suffer this way. An innocent man was treated like a criminal and unjustly punished, and yet it was God's good plan?

What are your thoughts on that?

Jesus knew God's purpose—that many people would be considered righteous because he took their sins (from verse 11)—and submitted himself to it. God delivered the people of Israel from Egyptians and Babylonians in the Old Testament. But an "exodus" continues today because Jesus redeemed us from bondage to sin.

What newness of life and joy have you experienced because of your own "exodus" from pain, shame, brokenness, and so much more?

A life that has been made new is free from shame or guilt. There isn't one of us who is not broken when we come to Jesus. *Everyone* has sinned, and we all have fallen short of God's perfect standard (see Romans 3:23).

> We come broken. Jesus takes our brokenness. We come guilty. Jesus takes our penalty. We come in bondage. Jesus sets us free.

REDEMPTION

The verses from Isaiah 53 above describe the price Jesus paid for our redemption. Redemption is a word people may toss around in church, but we might not clearly understand. Let's unpack it a little. When we redeem something, we exchange it for something else. When we redeem a coupon, we exchange it for a discount. When we redeem a winning ticket, we exchange it for the prize. When we redeem aluminum cans, we exchange them for something of value—money. When we redeem a pawned diamond ring, we buy it back.

When Jesus redeems us, he exchanges our broken life for new life. He exchanges our debt and the penalty of our sin—death—for the promise of eternal life. He purchased freedom from the bondage of sin by paying the ultimate price with his life.

What other words come to mind when you think of redemption (redeemed)?

When we fix something broken, it may not be perfect, but it's re-made just the same. Likewise, we may still have scars, but instead of bringing shame, they speak of God's greatness.

The scars from our brokenness are evidence of healing—shadows of the scars Jesus wears because he exchanged his life for ours. Our imperfections tell of the glory and greatness of our God, who is more powerful than the grave and strong enough to break the bonds of darkness.

BROKENNESS

Those healed places have such rich meaning when we think how they point others to Christ. Let's look at Isaiah again.

Our brokenness is not more than God's greatness!

> To all who mourn in Israel,
> he will give a crown of beauty for ashes,
> a joyous blessing instead of mourning,
> festive praise instead of despair.
> In their righteousness, they will be like great oaks
> that the Lord has planted for his own glory. (Isaiah 61:3)

This paints a beautiful picture of how Jesus provides a way for us to have a restored relationship with God—made right, or righteous.

What comes to mind when you think of a big oak tree?

Like giant oak trees that grow from a tiny seed planted in the ground, we are to grow up in Christ and display God's glory, pointing others toward his greatness.

In his own words, Jesus said, "I tell you the truth, unless a kernel of wheat is planted in the soil and dies, it remains alone. But its death will produce many new kernels—a plentiful harvest of new lives" (John 12:24).

Here, he used a common illustration that people then and now could understand. If you've ever planted a seed for a flower or vegetable, have you really looked at the speck of dead kernel? It's hard to believe anything will come of it. But from that seed being buried in the soil, it produces another fruit-bearing plant. Jesus showed a word picture of his death and resurrection. One commentary explained it this way: "He, the Son of God and the Son of man, would conquer the destroyer of life—death—and thereby guarantee the life of man beyond the grave."[*]

Jesus knew that he would produce something greater through his death. Likewise, when we give our brokenness to God, he produces something greater than we could ever imagine.

In giving us joy and beauty and praise through our pain, he also plants us like big oak trees to testify to who he is.

What have you surrendered to God and buried along with your before-you-knew-Jesus self that now stands like a tall oak that testifies of grace and redemption?

As I was writing this book, I retreated to a cabin at a place called Oak Shores Resort. The tall oaks provided a sense of being in a cathedral. "The oak is often a symbol of strength. As a venerable, mighty tree, the oak is associated with worship (Gen. 13:18), with sacrificial offerings (Hos. 4:13), long life (Isa. 6:13), and sanctuaries ('the oak in the sanctuary of the Lord' at Shechem, Josh. 24:26)."[**]

[**] Susan Rattray, "Oak," in *The HarperCollins Bible Dictionary* (Revised and Updated), ed. Mark Allan Powell (New York: HarperCollins, 2011), 712.

[*] Harvey J. S. Blaney, "The Gospel According to St. John," in Matthew-Acts, vol. 4, *The Wesleyan Bible Commentary* (Grand Rapids, MI: William B. Eerdmans Publishing Company, 1966), 433.

Jesus was broken so we might experience freedom. He used bread and wine when he tried to explain this significance to his disciples. "For I pass on to you what I received from the Lord himself. On the night when he was betrayed, the Lord Jesus took some bread and gave thanks to God for it. Then he broke it in pieces and said, 'This is my body, which is given for you. Do this in remembrance of me'" (1 Corinthians 11:23–24).

Think of the last time you took communion at church (also called the Lord's Supper and the Eucharist). What made it meaningful for you?

Why do you think Jesus used something as common as bread and wine to demonstrate his sacrifice?

It hurts to be broken, doesn't it? Many of us turn to unhealthy behaviors to numb the pain of our broken hearts, but these things will never heal our brokenness: drugs, alcohol, food, shopping, perfectionism, promiscuity, lying, bitterness, anger, cutting, over-controlling, over-pleasing. Many of us struggle—some of us in secret—and maybe we're unaware that we turn to a behavior because it's a habit that comes so naturally to us.

What's your vice when you feel broken?

Ask yourself, "Am I brokenhearted today?" Listen to the hope we find in Psalms. "The LORD is close to the brokenhearted; he rescues those whose spirits are crushed" (Psalm 34:18). "He heals the brokenhearted and bandages their wounds" (Psalm 147:3).

What picture do these verses give you of God's care for you?

JESUS SEES YOUR HURT

Do you feel abandoned? Are you hiding scars? Jesus sees them and understands them. He had scars too. God the Father is near, and he desires to care for your heart wounds.

 When we come humbly to God with our hearts truly broken about our sin, he will not turn us away! That tender ache in our hearts might be there because we're ready for the healing only he provides.

> *The sacrifice you desire is a broken spirit. You will not reject a broken and repentant heart, O God.* —Psalm 51:17

Have you noticed that when you're hurting, your heart is most tender and receptive to having God bring about a change? Why do you think that is?

Why is it more difficult to experience change or repentance (turning around to a new direction) when everything is going our way?

In order to repair us, Jesus broke one thing that will forever remain broken—the power of sin.

> We know that our old sinful selves were crucified with Christ so that sin might lose its power in our lives. We are no longer slaves to sin. For when we died with Christ we were set free from the power of sin. And since we died with Christ, we know we will also live with him. We are sure of this because Christ was raised from the dead, and he will never die again. Death no longer has any power over him. When he died, he died once to break the power of sin. But now that he lives, he lives for the glory of God. So you also should consider yourselves to be dead to the power of sin and alive to God through Christ Jesus. (Romans 6:6–11)

What does being "dead to the power of sin" mean to you?

He wants us to experience the beauty and joy of a life that has been redeemed!

What does it mean to be "alive to God through Christ Jesus"?

We can experience this victory because of Jesus's victory. If others broke our hearts, he understands. If our hearts are broken because of our own choices, he gives us the opportunity to press the reset button and start over, completely forgiven. He wants us to experience the beauty and joy of a life that has been redeemed!

What "reset button" are you ready for Jesus to press?

Prayer Journal

I'M THANKFUL FOR:

_____

_____

_____

_____

_____

I'M ASKING GOD FOR:

_____

_____

_____

_____

_____

WORDS OF WORSHIP TO GOD:

_____

_____

_____

_____

_____

APPLY

MICRO STUDY 1

Read Isaiah 43:1–7.

Write out Isaiah 43:1 here:

_____

_____

_____

_____

_____

_____

_____

_____

_____

In this verse, Jacob is a reference to Israel. Because the Lord has created, formed, ransomed (redeemed), and called his people, they are his. God has a special relationship with his covenant people. Even though we aren't the ones this passage was written specifically to, we can learn something about God here. What do you learn about his nature?

Despite all the times they faced God's wrath, he still called them his chosen people. Describe how God's love for Israel encourages you as well.

Jesus said, "For even the Son of Man came not to be served but to serve others and to give his life as a ransom for many" (Matthew 20:28). What does it mean to you to be counted among the "many" that Jesus gave his life to redeem?

My prayer to God today is:

_____

_____

_____

_____

_____

_____

_____

_____

_____

_____

_____

_____

_____

MICRO STUDY 2

Write out Isaiah 43:2:

_____

_____

_____

_____

_____

_____

_____

_____

If you've read any part of the Old Testament, you know that the people of Israel went through deep waters and rivers of difficulty and then some. God committed to care for them. What "deep waters" have you been through?

Jesus said, "What is the price of two sparrows—one copper coin? But not a single sparrow can fall to the ground without your Father knowing it. And the very hairs on your head are all numbered. So don't be afraid; you are more valuable to God than a whole flock of sparrows" (Matthew 10:29–31). How does this passage make you feel?

Do you struggle with brokenness? What is your go-to comfort? (Shopping, alcohol, drugs, lying, food, bitterness, etc.)

What story does God want to tell with your life? Where has God shown you that he was with you all the way?

My prayer to God today is:

_____

_____

_____

_____

_____

_____

_____

_____

_____

_____

_____

MICRO STUDY 3

Write out Isaiah 43:3–5 here:

_____

_____

_____

_____

_____

_____

_____

_____

_____

_____

The passage talks about the Lord gathering his exiled children from places such as Assyria and Babylonia, those who ended up in captivity because they chose to disobey him.* If you've wandered away from the safety of God's freedom and into bondage, just like the people of Israel, reflect on how God gathers his own and brings them back to himself.

Imagine him reaching out and gathering you into his arms. What does that feel like?

---

* See also Isaiah 11:11–12 and Psalm 107:3.

Jesus mourned over the salvation of the Jews, saying he longed to gather them as a hen would gather chicks beneath her wings to protect them, but they refused (Matthew 23:37). God gave them free will—they could choose that protection or reject it.

When have you refused the safety Jesus offered to you and pursued your own path? How did it work out?

What happened when you surrendered to God's care and protection over your heart, mind, and body?

My prayer to God today is:

_____

_____

_____

_____

_____

_____

_____

_____

_____

_____

_____

_____

MICRO STUDY 4

Write out Isaiah 43:6–7 here:

_____

_____

_____

_____

_____

_____

_____

_____

_____

_____

_____

_____

_____

The promise was for God's chosen people, Israel, but as those redeemed by Jesus Christ, we also receive this promise that God has called us by name, ransomed us, and created us for his glory.
What is your deepest heart pain? What needs healing right now?

What has been healed so that you might rejoice?

What does it say to you that God has called you by name?

What does it mean to have been created for his glory?

My prayer to God today is:

_____

_____

_____

_____

_____

_____

_____

_____

_____

_____

_____

_____

MICRO STUDY 5

Read Psalm 107:1–9.

Write out verses 8–9 here:

_____

_____

_____

_____

_____

_____

_____

_____

_____

If you have returned to the Lord after wandering, you have a beautiful story to tell! There is freedom from shame for those who are redeemed. Who needs to hear your story? Who might you encourage?

Write part of your story here and consider sharing a short version of it with a friend in the next week.

_____

_____

_____

_____

_____

My prayer to God today is:

Hope in Action

IF YOU WOULD LIKE A PHYSICAL REMINDER of how God turns our pain into something beautiful, you might create a necklace pendant.

+ Pick up a glass vial pendant, a chain, and your favorite color of glitter (sold at a craft or hobby supply store).

+ On a small piece of paper, write down the pain that you'd like to find beauty in.

+ Carefully burn that piece of paper in the fireplace or over a campfire, and then, when the ashes are completely cooled, mix a tiny amount of ash with glitter and place it in the glass pendant.

When you look at this necklace, be reminded that Jesus came to turn our mourning into joy and beauty. We can find beauty in the ashes.

WEEK TWO
RESTART

This means that anyone who belongs to Christ has become a new person. The old life is gone; a new life has begun!
—2 Corinthians 5:17

First Thoughts

BEFORE WE START, TAKE A FEW MINUTES to write and reflect, using the space provided for notes. Use the journal writing prompts to think about what it means to restart.

- I remember starting over with _____.

- When I have to start over, I feel _____
  _____.

- I'm so glad I got a second chance to _____
  _____.

- Some things that come to mind when I hear the word failure
  are _____.

_____

_____

_____

_____

_____

_____

_____

_____

_____

_____

_____

STORY

LAST WEEK, WE STUDIED WHAT IT MEANS to be redeemed—set free because Jesus exchanged his life for ours. As we begin this week, let's think about what it means to restart. Recall a time in your life when you started something over or think of something you wished you could start over.

I once started my piece in a piano recital, and then it quickly crashed and burned when my fingers shifted off the correct position. The lights bore down on me at the keys, and I kept playing. Thank goodness my back was to the audience, but I didn't know what to do. Instead of beautiful music, what came from my fingers on the keys sounded much more like an out-of-tune piano abandoned in someone's basement.

At last, I stopped.

For her younger students, my kind and wonderful teacher would stand just off to the side of the grand piano during the recital. She was out of the shot for photo opportunities but within eyesight of nervous students. I looked her way.

"Can I start over?"

She nodded the reassurance I needed.

I'm certain someone in the crowd must have sighed in relief, "Yes, praise Jesus. Let her start over!"

I started from the top.

The song? I'll never forget it. *Nobody Knows the Trouble I've Seen.*

Nobody knows the trouble of a nervous pianist.

Maybe your do-over was a presentation or an interview. Maybe there was an exam you retook. Maybe you painted a whole room, but it looked like a baby poop explosion, and you went back to the paint store for a better shade.

Starting over might be a good thing or a bad thing. It might produce relief or frustration. It all depends on the circumstances!

BUYER'S REMORSE

Have you ever purchased something you thought was wonderful, only to find it in a pile of neglected stuff a few years later? If so, you may have wondered, *What was I thinking when I bought this?*

Odds are, we all have owned one of those crazy things that we once loved but ended up donating to a thrift store, putting on a garage sale, or repurposing in some other way. Sometimes we just toss these items in the trash. And sometimes we look for someone to pawn our purchase off on. Let the record show that this is not the way to endear yourself to most of your friends!

At the moment of purchase, we probably thought these eventual castoffs were the best thing ever. We thought we *had* to have it. Maybe it was the perfect outfit, or it was a gadget that you couldn't live without. It was never going to go out of fashion, or everyone else was getting one. Or so you thought.

For me, there was the Salad Shooter that I barely used until I discovered how well it could shred cheese. Forget that it could process healthy green things. Cheese was all that mattered.

Then there were the synthetic leather pants I had to have—remember pleather? I'd found them on a super-cheap sale rack for one dollar and wore them for a speaking event. Rivulets of sweat ran down my legs because they were stifling—like wearing hip waders but much more chic.

Purchases such as clothing and gadgets aren't the only causes of buyer's remorse. This happens with bigger life choices too. We start out headed in one direction but end up in another. Sometimes we spend four (or five, or six) long years in college, get licensed and certified, and set up twenty-five-year payment plans on student loans—only to discover we aren't happy with the career we chose before our hormones quit raging and the colossal zit on our face before senior prom was our biggest hardship.

When you were a kid or a young adult, what did you tell people you wanted to become? Think back to what your answer was. How has your thinking changed since then? Sometimes we feel 100 percent sure of something, only to discover later that our feelings misguided us. Or sometimes, we find that God has chosen a new direction for us, and the place we believed to be our destination was simply a stepping stone.

Unfortunately, we don't always get it right! That doesn't excuse anything if we make foolish decisions, but it does help us to understand. Most of us do not *intentionally* head in the wrong direction. We don't deliberately make a mistake that forces us to restart or purposely spend a ton of money on something that we will hate in a few years. We don't plan to take out student loans and make payments for decades to get a career we have walked away from before that debt is paid. Sometimes unexpected changes come along the way.

Sometimes, we simply missed the signs. We were sure that we were making the right choices, following all the rules, and yet, we missed the truth. We may have had the wrong information, or we hadn't thought things all the way through, or we failed to consult God.

Sometimes, we end up in a place far from where God wants us to be, and we wonder, *How did I get here?*

Now imagine what it would feel like if you were sure that you were in the right career, you followed all the rules, and were committed to God's will. And suddenly, you discovered that you'd been blind to the truth.

That is what happened to Saul (Paul) in the story we will study in the rest of this book.

PRAYER

HEAVENLY FATHER, WE WANT TO KNOW THE truth and be directed by that truth. Open our eyes so we can understand your heart and act as you would want us to act. Reveal where we have blind spots and need to make changes or amends. We ask that you give us the willingness to forgive and experience the freedom that comes from letting go of regret. Help us to be sensitive to others and caring, with hearts full of your love and grace. Thank you for giving each of us a restart. Thank you for your love and the grace you give us every day. Amen.

EXPLORE THE WORD

THE APOSTLE PAUL STARTED OUT AS A zealous follower of the Scriptures—to the point of legalism. Paul is an example of how something well-intentioned can lead us far from the truth.

In the New Testament book of Acts, we see the beginning of the

Sanhedrin (Greek *synedrion*; Hebrew, *sanhedrin*). The supreme council in charge of Jewish affairs in Roman Palestine. According to *The Lexham Bible Dictionary*, "While the exact makeup and nature of the Jewish governing body in first-century Palestine is uncertain, the varying depictions of the Sanhedrin reveal a group consisting of priests and religious teachers who meet to decide on legal matters with religious, political, and social ramifications."[*]

---

[*] Douglas Mangum and Vasile Babota, "Sanhedrin," in *The Lexham Bible Dictionary*, ed. John D. Barry et al. (Bellingham, WA: Lexham Press, 2016).

Was Saul's name changed to Paul when he became a Christian?

Saul was known more in Scripture as the apostle Paul but was also known by his Jewish name of Saul of Tarsus, even after the encounter with Jesus. Acts 13:9 says, "Saul, also known as Paul." There is no specific mention in Scripture that Jesus changed his name, although many Bible teachers have stated this. Paul was born in Tarsus (on the southern coast of modern-day Turkey).*

He was schooled as a Pharisee (Acts 23:6; 26:5). He mentioned his Jewish heritage several times: 2 Cor. 11:22; Phil. 3:4–5; and Rom. 11:1 (from the tribe of Benjamin).

When Paul became a traveling missionary for Jesus and a preacher, he may have chosen to use his Roman name, Paul, because of the territories he traveled in.

---

* Anthony Le Donne, "Paul the Apostle," in *The Lexham Bible Dictionary*, ed. John D. Barry et al. (Bellingham, WA: Lexham Press, 2016).

Christian church. There were a lot of wonderful things happening, and the church was growing like crazy. The good news of the gospel spread quickly, and thousands of people chose to follow Jesus.

Though the followers of Jesus performed miracles just as he did, there were many challenges for these early Christians, including persecution. The Christians had set out to do the right thing and to spread the gospel but were met with resistance from Jewish religious leaders. Their very lives were in danger.

In Acts 6 and 7, we are introduced to Stephen, one of the Jewish Christians.

What do you know about Stephen from stories or sermons in the past?

Stephen was a powerful evangelist for the gospel of Jesus, and the Jewish leaders felt threatened by this (Acts 6:9). So, they came up with a way to entrap Stephen.

> So they persuaded some men to lie about Stephen, saying, "We heard him blaspheme Moses, and even God." This roused the people, the elders, and the teachers of religious law. So they arrested Stephen and brought him before the high council. (Acts 6:11–12)

The high council was called the Sanhedrin. Think of this as the Jewish Supreme Court. This was the same court that had condemned Jesus to crucifixion, and now they were after Jesus's followers.

In his testimony in Acts 7, Stephen accused the members of the high court of being heathen and deaf to the truth because they had rejected the gospel (v. 51). I can't help but wonder: *What was he thinking? Didn't he realize the consequences?*

What kind of boldness do you think it took for Stephen to be able to challenge the Sanhedrin this way?

Are you someone who typically speaks up when you see something wrong, or do you prefer to stay quiet?

The accusation made the rulers so furious they shook their fists at Stephen. "Then they put their hands over their ears and began shouting. They rushed at him and dragged him out of the city and began to stone him. His accusers took off their coats and laid them at the feet of a young man named Saul" (Acts 7:57–58).

Did you just picture them covering their ears and shouting non-sense to shut out the truth? There could have been a meme for that in Jewish social media—Scrollbook. (Didn't know you know the Jews had social media back then?)

REFUSING TO HEAR THE TRUTH

Put yourself in this situation for a moment. Have you ever dealt with someone who refused to hear the truth? How did you feel?

(*continued*)

His missionary work started with the Jews but progressed into Gentile areas.* But there is no proof that Paul was his Christian name.

"The book of Acts continues to call him Saul some fifteen years into his life as a Christian, only suddenly to switch to Paul while he is on the island of Cyprus (Acts 13:9). The best explanation of Paul's dual names is that one of these is his nickname, and the other is part of his name as a Roman citizen."†

He also mentioned in Acts 22 that he was a Roman citizen by birth, which alarmed the commander of a company of Roman soldiers that had captured Paul. It is unclear how Paul or his parents obtained citizenship.

---

* John D. Barry et al., *Faithlife Study Bible* (Bellingham, WA: Lexham Press, 2012, 2016), Ac 13:9.

† Kenneth Schenck, *Paul: Messenger of Grace* (Indianapolis, IN: WPH, 2010), 25.

This refusal to listen isn't like what we do when someone shares TMI (too much information) and we don't want to hear it. This is a serious problem of the high court refusing to hear the truth.

Why is that concerning?

As the accusers rushed at Stephen to put him to death unjustly, there was a young man in their group—a Pharisee who was diligent in his studies. They took off their coats as they prepared to murder Stephen, and they laid their coats at the feet of a man named Saul.

> Saul was one of the witnesses, and he agreed completely with the killing of Stephen. A great wave of persecution began that day, sweeping over the church in Jerusalem; and all the believers except the apostles were scattered through the regions of Judea and Samaria. (Some devout men came and buried Stephen with great mourning.) But Saul was going everywhere to destroy the church. He went from house to house, dragging out both men and women to throw them into prison. (Acts 8:1–3)

Let's pause here. We might assume Saul was a terrible man. Don't get me wrong. His actions were certainly terrible! Perhaps you've heard Sunday school stories of Saul.

Describe any perceptions you have of Saul based on what you have learned in the past.

Let's look at who Saul was and how he started on this journey of persecuting Christians. He was not an atheist. He did not deny the existence of God.

Wait. Did you get that?

Saul believed in God.

I don't know about you, but I often thought of him as similar to Attila the Hun, a barbarian invader whom Christian authors refer to as the "Scourge of God."* However, Saul was a young man who had started off on a path that he thought was the right one. As a Pharisee, he was part of an influential religious group within Judaism.

Saul said, "As the Jewish leaders are well aware, I was given a thorough Jewish training from my earliest childhood among my own people and in Jerusalem. If they would admit it, they know that I have been a member of the Pharisees, the strictest sect of our religion" (Acts 26:4–5).

Pharisees were known for their emphasis on holiness—being set apart—and on being devoutly religious. As a Pharisee, Saul would have been focused on the tradition of the written law of the Old Testament and on observing every microscopic point of that law. The problem with the Pharisees was that their focus was all wrong. It was on legalism.

The Pharisees accepted Scripture as inspired by God. At the time of Saul, they would have had the Old Testament writings available to them for study. The problem with their traditions was that they had added to Scripture, and their man-made traditions had become as important to them as God's Word. And in the name of truth, they murdered people.

How can this be a caution for us in our own Christian faith?

> The Pharisees had a tradition of a strict interpretation of the Law of Moses and had added many extensions to the law that were designed to maintain religious identity and purity. The term "Pharisee" comes from the Aramaic word prsh, which means "to separate," "divide," or "distinguish."**

** Bradley T. Johnson, "Pharisees," in *The Lexham Bible Dictionary*, ed. John D. Barry et al. (Bellingham, WA: Lexham Press, 2016).

* Sharon Rusten with E. Michael, *The Complete Book of When & Where in the Bible and throughout History* (Wheaton, IL: Tyndale House Publishers, Inc., 2005), 133.

What might cause you to become so passionate about something that you'd miss the truth?

How destructive is it when Christian leaders refuse to hear truth?

SEPARATING TRUTH FROM TRADITIONS

Eventually, it became difficult to separate the truth from all the traditions and practices that had been added to it. Perhaps you've experienced this.

Name something you do because you've always done it that way (even if you don't know why).

There is an old fable I've heard that goes something like this. A woman is preparing a ham for Easter dinner. She cuts the ends off the meat before putting it in the pan. Her daughter, who is watching, asks, "Why do you do that?"

Mom answers, "Because my mother always did it that way."

Not satisfied with the response, the daughter wonders why it should be done this way. So, when her grandmother arrives for dinner, she asks her why she did this. Grandmother says, "Because my mother always did it that way."

Still unsatisfied, the girl turns to her great-grandmother, who is also seated at the table, and repeats the question.

"Oh, that's easy, dear. I never had a big enough pan, so I always cut the ends off to make it fit."

Identify some religious traditions that you practice and for which you can't find biblical commands requiring them.

If you grew up folding your hands and bowing your head when praying before a meal, you have one of those traditions. Jesus gave thanks before breaking bread, but I don't recall a mention of folding hands or closing eyes at the last supper. I suspect someone started the tradition somewhere to keep Timmy from stealing a chicken leg while his papa said the blessing, and the practice stuck.

When God's laws became mixed with a heap of man-made rules and traditions, many religious people didn't understand the difference. They performed rituals like robots following orders without questioning them. Jesus condemned the practices of the Pharisees.

> Jesus replied, "You hypocrites! Isaiah was right when he prophesied about you, for he wrote, 'These people honor me with their lips, but their hearts are far from me. Their worship is a farce, for they teach man-made ideas as commands from God.' For you ignore God's law and substitute your own tradition." Then he said, "You skillfully sidestep God's law in order to hold on to your own tradition." (Mark 7:6–9)

What did Jesus say about the Pharisees and religious teachers to their faces?

What has been your understanding of the word *hypocrite*?

Jesus told his disciples not to follow the example of the teachers of the religious law and the Pharisees. He said, "The teachers of religious law and the Pharisees are the official interpreters of the law of Moses. So practice and obey whatever they tell you, but don't follow their example. For they don't practice what they teach. They crush people with unbearable religious demands and never lift a finger to ease the burden. Everything they do is for show. On their arms they wear extra wide prayer boxes with Scripture verses inside, and they wear robes with extra long tassels" (Matthew 23:2–5).

What religious practices might Christians of today do just for show?

The teachers of religious law and the Pharisees didn't practice what they taught. They based their religion on performance and showing off. They'd have been the ones who carried giant Bibles to church, plastered Bible verses on the walls of their offices, and insisted on leading a prayer before the softball game—all while consuming pornography behind closed doors—if they had lived in our century.

Religious performance looks good on the outside, puts on a show, and pretends we don't sin. It means we never let others see our authentic selves. When we act "religiously," without any actual spiritual change happening behind the pretense, we run the risk of hurting others.

How does religious performance place heavy burdens on people?

TRUTH AND GRACE

We talked in the last chapter about scars and wounds. Some of you have experienced hurt in the church. I want you to know my heart breaks for you. Jesus was direct when pointing out the need for repentance, but he never condemned those who came to him for hope and healing. He presented truth **and** grace.

Jesus told the Pharisees they were blind because they couldn't see the truth in front of them. He said he came "to give sight to the blind and to show those who think they see that they are blind" (John 9:39).

What does it mean to "*think* they see"?

We would certainly know if we were physically blind. Why is it so hard to "see" when we're spiritually blind?

Jesus warned his followers in John 16:1–3 that the time was coming when they would be killed for their faith by people who thought they were "doing a holy service for God." The Pharisees would be among those killing followers of Jesus.

As a Pharisee, Saul thought he could "see," but his religious pride caused a spiritual blindness that he was too ignorant to perceive. All he could see was the tradition in which he was raised and the narrow vision he thought was the right one. He needed a restart.

In the next study, we will learn that it took physical blindness for Saul to see his spiritual blindness. But for now, let's focus on this: there are times when someone's spiritual blindness causes them to crush the spirit of someone else.

When have you felt crushed by someone who might not have intended to hurt you? Maybe it was a teacher, a leader, or a boss.

Describe how it felt to experience this.

How did you respond?

How have you found healing since then?

Churches and Christian organizations are made up of humans. And humans get off track. Please hear that I'm not excusing or condoning spiritual abuse. And I strongly disapprove of handling abuse internally or sweeping it under the rug. There are no excuses.

Here, let's try to get at the root of where some hurt begins before it becomes abuse. And let's examine some of the ways legalism is so off-base. Sometimes we practice traditions without understanding the true meaning behind them.

Before Saul could begin to live the life that God would soon call him to live, he had to acknowledge that the way he practiced religion was way off track. His performance-based religion was nothing like the relationship Jesus offered.

The best part of Saul's story is that God chose him *even though* he was off track. God could have chosen anyone to bring the gospel around the world, but he chose Saul. God performed a dramatic change in him. This provides hope that God can change us too!

Now that you think of Saul's story from this perspective, what comes to mind?

We will continue with more of Saul's story in our next lesson, but for now, let's consider how this part of Saul's story applies to our lives.

If you have been hurt by someone who acted like a Pharisee, there is something you need to know. You may never experience an apology from someone who acted hurtfully in the name of religion. They might never receive the "sight" required to overcome their pride and admit they wronged you. But you can find healing, despite the injustice. You can go from a victim to someone living in spiritual victory!

Yes, this means being vulnerable. It means opening your heart to be real with someone who is safe. You have value, purpose, gifts and abilities, courage, and confidence. You have so much to offer to others when you step from behind the mask of a victim. You can have a restart too.

Jesus experienced the ultimate spiritual abuse so that we could experience the ultimate spiritual freedom—from even this!

What encouragement does this give you?

What freedom have you found in releasing past hurts, even though you've never received an apology?

This truth is also for the Sauls out there. If you have acted like a Pharisee and hurt someone else, it isn't too late to make amends. Maybe you don't even know what you've done.

> You may never experience an apology from someone who acted hurtfully in the name of religion. . . . But you can find healing, despite the injustice.

Remember, the Pharisees started out as well-meaning people. They studied the law and knew it as well as anyone. It was the attitude of their hearts that was the problem. They were self-righteous and hypocritical.

When is it difficult for you to accept that you might be wrong about something?

Be transparent, vulnerable, honest, and humble in considering how your own thoughts and actions might be rooted in legalism or pride. I say this because God has been uprooting those for years in my heart too.

You also have so much to offer to others. Imagine how effective your life might be if a sense of love and empathy were transparent to those around you! Ask God to open your eyes to areas needing change.

God offers the same love and forgiveness for all who turn from their sin and follow the truth. Today, we pray for healing for both those who have hurt others and for those who have been hurt. Let us all restart in Jesus!

What is God impressing on your heart after today's study?

Prayer Journal

I'M THANKFUL FOR:

_____

_____

_____

_____

_____

_____

I'M ASKING GOD FOR:

_____

_____

_____

_____

_____

_____

WORDS OF WORSHIP TO GOD:

_____

_____

_____

_____

_____

_____

APPLY

MICRO STUDY 1

Read Ephesians 2:1–5, an excerpt from a letter the apostle Paul (Saul) wrote.

Write out verses 4–5 here:

_____

_____

_____

_____

_____

_____

_____

_____

_____

_____

Why do you think God chose one who was once such an enemy of his people to be such a great teacher and the church's greatest missionary to the Gentiles?

What did Paul describe as God's motive for giving us a restart?

Paul was so extreme with his legalistic views that he missed the big picture. God intervened and gave him an opportunity for a restart. Write about your restart story. How have you seen your life change since you started following Jesus?

My prayer to God today is:

_____

_____

_____

_____

_____

_____

_____

_____

_____

_____

_____

MICRO STUDY 2

Read Ephesians 2:6–9.

Write out verse 9 here:

_____

_____

_____

_____

_____

Saul (Paul) did such terrible things, persecuting Christians in the past. Therefore, how was his restart an example of the incredible wealth of God's grace?

Have you ever labeled yourself as hopeless, thinking God doesn't have enough grace for you?

What does it mean to you to be united with Christ Jesus?

How did Paul's life prove that salvation is not a reward for our good deeds?

What about your current habits or beliefs would make it seem as if you believed you could earn God's favor by being good?

How would you explain grace to someone who didn't understand it?

My prayer to God today is:

_____

_____

_____

_____

_____

_____

_____

_____

_____

MICRO STUDY 3

Read Ephesians 2:10–13.

Write out verse 10 here:

_____

_____

_____

_____

_____

_____

Describe a situation in which you thought you were right but then later discovered you were wrong. What did you do when you discovered you were wrong?

Paul noted that the Gentiles were once taunted by the Jews as heathens and outsiders. Paul would know since he was one of those who did the taunting. But now he was passionate about reaching out to the Gentiles with good news.

What did Paul say here about the inclusiveness of the gospel?

> Although all people are alienated from God because of sin, the Gentiles were what has been called "double alienated" because they were also alienated from God's people.*

---

* John R. W. Stott, *God's New Society: The Message of Ephesians, The Bible Speaks Today* (Downers Grove, IL: InterVarsity Press, 1979), 92.

Good works are the result of salvation—not the cause of it. When grace transforms us and renews us, we become motivated to do good things. Describe the difference between being obligated to do good things to earn something and being motivated because of receiving something.

Don't miss the "but now" in verse 13. It's the pivotal moment in a re-start. It's when we used to be one way, but now we are another. Write out your own statement:

I used to be _____

_____, but now I _____

_____

_____ because of Jesus.

Additional thoughts:

My prayer to God today is:

_____

_____

_____

_____

_____

_____

_____

_____

_____

_____

MICRO STUDY 4

Read Ephesians 2:14–18.

Write out verse 18 here:

_____

_____

_____

_____

_____

_____

Describe the kind of peace Paul is talking about in verse 14.

If you were wounded by someone claiming to be a Christian, how do you feel about knowing there is hope for healing and change?

Notice how Jesus removed the dividing labels (Jew and Gentile) and created one new group of people—one body. Describe the social and religious practices that divide people today.

"The Jew had an immense contempt for the Gentile. The Gentiles, said the Jews, were created by God to be fuel for the fires of hell. God, they said, loves only Israel of all the nations that he had made . . . It was not even lawful to render help to a Gentile mother in her hour of sorest need, for that would simply be to bring another Gentile into the world. Until Christ came, the Gentiles were an object of contempt to the Jews. The barrier between them was absolute. If a Jewish boy married a Gentile girl, or if a Jewish girl married a Gentile boy, the funeral of that Jewish boy or girl was carried out. Such contact with a Gentile was the equivalent of death."
—William Barclay*

---

* William Barclay, *The Letters to the Galatians and Ephesians in the Daily Study Bible* (The Saint Andrew Press, 1954. 2nd edition, 1958) 125, as quoted in John R. W. Stott, *God's New Society: The Message of Ephesians, The Bible Speaks Today* (Downers Grove, IL: InterVarsity Press, 1979), 91.

How might we restart—change our focus—to reclaim the unity Paul speaks of here?

Paul knew both sides of the hurt. First, he was the one persecuting. Then he became the one being persecuted. How do you think this affected how he felt toward outsiders?

What would it be like if you could forget the past and move forward? Write out a few sentences describing your state of mind and how you would *like* to feel or how you *do* feel as a result of God performing a miracle on your thoughts. Describe how it feels to be forgiven, healed of hurt, released from bitterness and anger, and living all-in as a follower of Christ.

My prayer to God today is:

_____

_____

_____

_____

_____

_____

MICRO STUDY 5

Read Ephesians 2:19–22.

Write out verses 19–20 here:

_____

_____

_____

_____

_____

_____

_____

_____

_____

What do you think it was like for Gentiles to be considered no longer strangers or foreigners but children of God, just like believing Jews?

What will your restart look like? Have you drifted away from church or withdrawn from participation because you didn't want to get hurt? Perhaps you feel alienated or spiritually homeless. Are you connected with God and people who love God, but you're not as fully invested in the relationships as you could be? Describe that.

"We need to get the failures of the church on our conscience, to feel the offence to Christ and the world which these failures are, to weep over the credibility gap between the church's talk and the church's walk, to repent of our readiness to excuse and even condone our failures, and to determine to do something about it. . . . Only then will the world believe in Christ as Peacemaker. Only then will God receive the glory due to his name."
—John R. W. Stott*

Paul described a sense of homelessness, as if they were once visitors with no legal rights. And then, he contrasted it with belonging, a complete change in position that comes with the rights of family. Describe what it means for you to be part of God's family.

My prayer to God today is:

_____

_____

_____

_____

_____

_____

_____

_____

_____

_____

* John R. W. Stott, *God's New Society: The Message of Ephesians,* The Bible Speaks Today (Downers Grove, IL: InterVarsity Press, 1979), 111–112.

Hope in Action

WRITE A LETTER TO SOMEONE YOU HURT or to someone who has hurt you.

Read the letter you wrote. How would you describe the tone if you were reading the words for the first time?

If you need to rewrite your letter to have a different tone, consider how you would write it if you truly wanted the best for that other person—this is what true love is. Write it without defensiveness, pride, or anger.

Pray about the contents of your letter, asking God for his healing for hurt or regret. Ask him what your next step should be.

For some, this process will be simply a therapeutic way to process your feelings. But for others, it might be the first step in a longer process of confronting, making amends, or forgiving. As you consider your next step, include the wisdom and feedback of a trusted leader or friend.

WEEK THREE
REPURPOSE

Don't copy the behavior and customs of this world, but let God transform you into a new person by changing the way you think. Then you will learn to know God's will for you, which is good and pleasing and perfect.
—Romans 12:2

First Thoughts

TAKE A FEW MOMENTS TO THINK ABOUT your before-and-after story.

How are you different now from how you once were? You can celebrate how you have grown and changed because of the power of God in your life!

The apostle Paul talked about what it meant to boast about his weakness. He knew that God produced the results in his life when God showed up with power, even when Paul was weak. It's important to stop occasionally to acknowledge what God has been working on in us and how he's still writing our testimony.

Write a free flow of the words that come to mind that describe the positive attitudes, actions, and attributes that God has produced in your life, even when you have felt inadequate and weak. If you have trouble seeing the Spirit's work in your life right now, write a prayer expressing your desire to the Lord to display his power.

_____

_____

_____

_____

_____

_____

_____

_____

_____

_____

STORY

IF YOU'RE A PINTEREST FAN OR A TikTok junkie, you might love stories that show a room or a piece of furniture before and after a transformation. The more awful the before picture and the more dramatic the after pictures, the more stunning the change. You've probably noticed that you have to see it to believe it too. If someone describes the change to you, that isn't nearly as effective as if you experience the change through photos, video, or in person.

As we think about before and after, think about something you have transformed or repurposed that you now love.

TRANSFORMED

Have you seen personal makeovers where someone gets a new hairstyle and designer clothes, but a few weeks later, they look a lot like their old self again? They have their ragged, baggy sweatpants and holey T-shirt on. No makeup. The once-voluminous, layered cut that triggered tears of joy now has no style. That isn't a transformation. That's a temporary change of outward appearance.

I'm not talking about the staged before and after weight loss photos either. You know, the ones where the person looks so unhappy in the before picture that it could be exchanged for a mug shot without anyone noticing?

Is there a photographer somewhere who does this work professionally?

"Ok now. Push your belly out. Look grumpy. Nope, that's too flattering. Put your arms by your sides. Stand like a linebacker. Good . . . Hold that." Click.

When something is transformed, it will never be the way it was again. When a *person* is transformed, they are changed from the inside out. Everything about them is changed.

If you were to repurpose an old wheelbarrow into a flower container, it would likely never haul bricks or concrete again. It resembles the shape of its former use, but its contents and purpose have been completely altered. If the wheel no longer rolls, it's ok—it doesn't need that wheel anymore. It now provides a place for radiant blooms to root and grow and bring joy to those who pass by.

If you use the pages of a vintage book as wallpaper for a room, it will never be read as a book again. If you repurpose a barn door as a tabletop, it will no longer be a barricade for sheep or goats. You get the idea. Something that is repurposed is also transformed.

When God changes us, we are no longer spiritually dead, but we are given new life and a new purpose.

Your before and your after stories might be dramatically different. The "before" picture might be one of incredible pain and difficulty. Your choices may have led you far from God's path. You might have been atheistic, apathetic, addicted, or angry—or something else that begins with *a* or any other letter in the alphabet. Apparently, I like alliteration. (There I go again with the letter *a*.)

Wherever you were or are, it doesn't have to be your forever story. God can dramatically repurpose any life.

Jesus chose disciples to be part of his ministry team, and he repurposed them from fishermen to ministers of the gospel. He taught them how to love God and love people and then gave them the task of building the foundations of the Christian church.

You are never so good that you don't need Jesus or so bad that he's unable to change you.

This week, we continue with the story of Saul, who had one of the most dramatic changes of all time.

> You are never so good that you don't need Jesus or so bad that he's unable to change you.

PRAYER

LORD, I KNOW YOU CAN DO SO much more than we could ever dream. I pray the words that Paul himself wrote in Ephesians 3:20–21: "Now all glory to God, who is able, through his mighty power at work within us, to accomplish infinitely more than we might ask or think. Glory to him in the church and in Christ Jesus through all generations forever and ever! Amen."

Thank you for those words, Lord. To you be glory in our friendships and in our homes. To you be glory in our work and in our recreation. We know you can do more than we could ever ask or imagine as you repurpose us. Amen.

EXPLORE THE WORD

SAUL HAD MADE IT HIS PERSONAL MISSION to hunt down, persecute, and imprison anyone who claimed to follow Jesus. His story is recorded in the book of Acts, which was written by Luke.

In the last study, I called him Saul. But because most of the New Testament refers to him by Paul, we will use that name from this point forward. I like backstory, so let's gather a little more of Paul's before we get to the repurposing. He grew up in a traditional Jewish home, but he wasn't born in Jerusalem to a well-established family of Jews. He was born in Tarsus,* which is a city in south-central Turkey located on the Tarsus River, about twelve miles from the Mediterranean Sea coast. There is a lot of speculation about how he received dual citizenship, but Paul never spelled it out.

Perhaps his citizenship was similar to if American parents were traveling in another country when their child was born. That child would have dual citizenship of the home country of the parents and of the country in which he was born. It's also possible his family had some connections to the Roman government in the province of Cilicia.

We established that Paul was educated as a Pharisee, and he was proud of his Jewish heritage, but it's also important to note that even after he changed, he still appreciated that heritage. I can relate to this in my own way. I no longer align doctrinally with the church I was part of until my mid-teen years. Yet I have high respect for the people who taught me and for the theology that launched me into asking questions and learning more about what the Bible says.

What part of your faith upbringing do you respect, even if you don't align with or adhere to it in the same way you were taught?

> **A little aside about Luke, the presumed writer of the book of Acts:**
>
> We don't know much about him, but we do know he was a physician and the only Gentile (a person who is not a Jew) to write any part of the New Testament. In his letter to the Colossians, Paul made a distinction between Luke and his other coworkers, and he called him "the beloved doctor" (see Colossians 4:14).

---

* See Acts 22.

One source said: "During this time of Pompey (67 BC), Tarsus was made the capital over the Roman province of Cilicia, and Jews began to receive Roman citizenship. Antony, who controlled the eastern provinces, declared the city free in 42 BC. Tarsus continued to receive special privileges under Augustus, who exempted the city from imperial taxation because Athenodorus, his teacher and friend, was a Tarsian. Tarsus grew into a cultural and intellectual center."* Although the dates don't perfectly align, perhaps this tied into Paul's citizenship. We don't know!

* "Tarsus," BiblePlaces.com, retrieved February 10, 2023, www.bibleplaces.com/tarsus.

Paul never forgot his Jewish upbringing. Later in life, when he wrote his story in a letter to the Philippians, he said, "I was circumcised when I was eight days old. I am a pure-blooded citizen of Israel and a member of the tribe of Benjamin—a real Hebrew if there ever was one! I was a member of the Pharisees, who demand the strictest obedience to the Jewish law. I was so zealous that I harshly persecuted the church. And as for righteousness, I obeyed the law without fault" (Philippians 3:5–6).

As we learned last week, persecuting Christians was Paul's way of showing his devotion—misguided though it was—to the Jewish law.

What stuck with you from last week's study about a restart?

What did you learn that was a newer idea for you?

DRAMATIC INTERRUPTION

Let's talk about this dramatic before and after that Paul went through. He was on his way to Damascus, carrying a letter from the high priest of the temple in Jerusalem that gave him authority to arrest anyone who followed Christ. Once when he told his story, Paul said, "I used to believe that I ought to do everything I could to oppose the very name of Jesus the Nazarene. Indeed, I did just that in Jerusalem. Authorized by the leading priests, I caused many believers there to be sent to prison. And I cast my vote against them when they were condemned to death. Many times I had them punished in the synagogues to get them to curse Jesus. I was so violently opposed to them that I even chased them down in foreign cities" (Acts 26:9–11).

Paul was going about his persecuting business when Jesus stepped into his path one day. Perhaps you're thinking, *Wait. Wasn't Jesus in heaven by this time?*

He certainly was, but it didn't stop him from interrupting Paul, and it certainly doesn't stop him from interrupting us either.

When has God interrupted your plans to get your attention?

Let's read how Paul told the story in Acts 26:12–19 when he was talking to King Agrippa.

> "One day I was on such a mission to Damascus, armed with the authority and commission of the leading priests. About noon, Your Majesty, as I was on the road, a light from heaven brighter than the sun shone down on me and my companions. We all fell down, and I heard a voice saying to me in Aramaic, 'Saul, Saul, why are you persecuting me? It is useless for you to fight against my will.'
>
> "'Who are you, lord?' I asked.
>
> "And the Lord replied, 'I am Jesus, the one you are persecuting. Now get to your feet! For I have appeared to you to appoint you as my servant and witness. Tell people that you have seen me, and tell them what I will show you in the future. And I will rescue you from both your own people and the Gentiles. Yes, I am sending you to the Gentiles to open their eyes, so they may turn from darkness to light and from the power of Satan to God.

As a later teen, I decided to be baptized to make a statement about choosing to follow Christ, even though I had been baptized as an infant. I wasn't negating or opposing what my parents chose for me when I was a newborn. In fact, I wanted to affirm their desire for me to follow Jesus and be fully committed to discipleship. Despite differences in theology, it was all part of my journey.

This is not to make a statement about which type of baptism any reader ought to practice but that we can see our heritage as part of the legacy of faith we build upon. Rather than arguing the fine points of doctrine, mutual respect for faith practices gets to the intent and purpose for the unity we share in Christ.

You can find Paul's story in three places in Acts:

Acts 9:1–9

Acts 22:6–11

Acts 26:9–20

Note that Jesus spoke to him in Aramaic (or some translations say Hebrew or Hebrew dialect).

Then they will receive forgiveness for their sins and be given a place among God's people, who are set apart by faith in me.'

"And so, King Agrippa, I obeyed that vision from heaven."

In another account of his story, we read that the men who were with Paul at the time of this encounter with God were speechless because they could hear a voice but couldn't see who was speaking. I don't know about you, but if Jesus spoke to me from heaven, I'd have no doubt he was serious.

And he spoke in the language of Paul's spiritual heritage—Aramaic. That's sort of like when a parent inserts a middle name to get our attention.

What do you think it would have been like to be one of Paul's companions that day?

Paul got up off the ground, and when he opened his eyes, he was blind. "So his companions led him by the hand to Damascus. He remained there blind for three days and did not eat or drink" (Acts 9:8–9).

The Lord sent a Christian man named Ananias to Paul to heal him.

"But Lord," exclaimed Ananias, "I've heard many people talk about the terrible things this man has done to the believers in Jerusalem! And he is authorized by the leading priests to arrest everyone who calls upon your name." But the Lord said, "Go, for Saul is my chosen instrument to take my message to the Gentiles and to kings, as well as to the people of Israel. And I will show him how much he must suffer for my name's sake." (Acts 9:13–16)

If you were Ananias, how would you have felt when God gave you this assignment?

When has God given you an "assignment" that made you say, "But Lord . . ."?

Paul's change was immediate. As soon as he regained his sight, he wanted to be baptized, a symbol of how Jesus had changed him and made him a new person. It was a dramatic makeover! It's similar to if a career criminal suddenly switched teams and became a police officer or a prosecuting attorney.

Imagine if you were someone who had known Paul before, and now he claimed to be playing for the other team. Would you have believed him?

Perhaps you know someone who has changed, and you're a bit skeptical, wondering if they might slip back into their old ways. Or maybe you're afraid of that person because you know the kinds of things they've done and the types of people they've hung out with.

Perhaps you have thought before that you've done too many "bad" things to have a chance at starting over. Paul's story offers hope to us all. There are no hopeless causes when we humbly come to God and receive the grace he offers.

Paul later said, "For I am the least of all the apostles. In fact, I'm not even worthy to be called an apostle after the way I persecuted God's church" (1 Corinthians 15:9).

What do you think he meant by saying he was the least of all?

When have you used those words about yourself: I'm not worthy?

Paul never forgot his "before" story. He understood the magnitude of what had happened. But it no longer defined him. He remembered what he *once* was and who he *now* was, and instead of dwelling on his past mistakes, he expressed incredible gratitude for how God changed him. He conveyed this in a letter to his colleague Timothy.

> I thank Christ Jesus our Lord, who has given me strength to do his work. He considered me trustworthy and appointed me to serve him, even though I used to blaspheme the name of Christ. In my insolence, I persecuted his people. But God had mercy on me because I did it in ignorance and unbelief. Oh, how generous and gracious our Lord was! He filled me with the faith and love that come from Christ Jesus.
>
> This is a trustworthy saying, and everyone should accept it: "Christ Jesus came into the world to save sinners"—and I am the worst of them all. But God had mercy on me so that Christ Jesus could use me as a prime example of his great patience with even the worst sinners. Then others will realize that they, too, can believe in him and receive eternal life. (1 Timothy 1:12–16)

What was Paul's new purpose there at the end of the passage?

Paul was willing to be an example, a before-and-after picture that would help others realize that they could also believe and have eternal life. He was repurposed!

What is your story? What amazing thing has God done to change you? Next week we will continue with Paul's story, but as we wrap up today, let's focus on what it means to live a repurposed life.

+ We have a new motivation.

+ We approach trials with a different mindset.

What motivates you? What passion has God put in your heart?

How has God changed your mindset about trials and challenges?

Paul's change was dramatic and instant. For some of us, it's more gradual. As God unveils something new, we apply that and change more, and then change again when he nudges us again. Please don't be discouraged if your progress isn't as drastic as Paul's or someone else's. This is about your journey and what God specifically wants for you.

As God transforms the way you think, it will change how you act. Paul wrote:

> And so, dear brothers and sisters, I plead with you to give your bodies to God because of all he has done for you. Let them be a living and holy sacrifice—the kind he will find acceptable. This is truly the way to worship him. Don't copy the behavior and customs of this world, but let God transform you into a new person by changing the way you think. Then you will learn to know God's will for you, which is good and pleasing and perfect. (Romans 12:1–2)

Your first step is surrender. Let God have control, so he can work on your thinking and change your motivation. As you discover his will, you can take the next step of obedience.

Let God have control, so he can work on your thinking and change your motivation.

What keeps you from full surrender right now?

What questions do you have that you'd like to explore more?

Prayer Journal

I'M THANKFUL FOR:

I'M ASKING GOD FOR:

WORDS OF WORSHIP TO GOD:

APPLY

MICRO STUDY 1

Read 2 Corinthians 5:1–10.

Write out verse 7 here:

_____

_____

_____

_____

The Bible talks about our before and after as dying to ourselves and being alive with eternal life in Christ. Our "death" is that of the old sinful nature. It was buried with Christ, and just as he was raised up by the Father, we are each raised up to live as a new person. Our earthly bodies are just temporary homes, ones with aches and pains at that.

What comfort do you find in knowing that your present struggles are part of living in an earthly body while you have a promise of something better to come?

"A 'guarantee' was used in Paul's time in commercial transactions; today the same Greek word is used for an engagement ring, pledging and guaranteeing the marriage day."
—Paul Barnett[*]

* Paul Barnett, *The Message of 2 Corinthians: Power in Weakness, The Bible Speaks Today* (Leicester, England; Downers Grove, IL: Inter-Varsity Press, 1988), 100.

In verse 5, Paul spoke of the Holy Spirit as a guarantee—like a deposit—on what is to come after this life. He had total confidence in the promise of life after death.

Paul left a lot of questions unanswered when it comes to the future age. What questions come to mind for you as you read this?

Perhaps you've seen verse 7 on coffee mugs and wall decorations, but what does living by faith mean? (See 2 Corinthians 4:18 and 1 Corinthians 13:12 for more ideas.)

If you were to fix your eyes *only* on the troubles you experience, how discouraging might that be for you compared with focusing on what Jesus promises for your eternal future?

What goal can you set based on verse 9?

My prayer to God today is:

_____

_____

_____

_____

_____

_____

_____

MICRO STUDY 2

Read 2 Corinthians 5:11–15.

Write out verse 15 here:

_____

_____

_____

_____

_____

_____

_____

_____

Because Paul had experienced the freedom he received, he wanted to give others the opportunity too. But that wasn't his only motive. God compelled him with love. He had a new purpose.

Describe the difference between sharing the gospel with someone because of love for them rather than a desire to shame them.

The people who knew Paul before were confused by the transformation. Who in your life doesn't understand your dedication to live for Christ? Which friends, family, or coworkers don't get it? How do you respond?

How do you think Paul felt about having this new purpose—showing people light and life—after his former purpose was killing and persecuting?

What concepts stand out most for you from what you have explored of Paul's story so far?

My prayer to God today is:

_____

_____

_____

_____

_____

_____

_____

_____

_____

MICRO STUDY 3

Read 2 Corinthians 5:16–17.

Write out verse 17 here:

_____

_____

_____

_____

_____

_____

_____

Here Paul talked about having a new view of people when we have new life in Jesus. Imagine how it would feel if your heart stopped and someone brought you back to life through CPR. How precious would every breath seem after that?

What would you change about your current life if you experienced that?

As a result of the change in us, God gives us a new mission and purpose in life. It isn't to live for ourselves or for temporary happiness. It's to be set apart—which is what *holy* means—to be ambassadors for Jesus. It's to live in a way that points people to him. Maybe you're afraid to talk about it because people are confused by the change in you, or they don't understand. Ask God for open doors in conversations to talk openly about the life Jesus offers. But know that showing it without words is highly effective as well.

In our study earlier of Acts 26:18, we read about God's purpose for Paul. God sent him to preach to people "to open their eyes, so they may turn from darkness to light and from the power of Satan to God. Then they will receive forgiveness for their sins." How would it feel to live in darkness, not understanding the truth?

How does it feel to live in light, having died to the darkness of your old life?

Write the name of one person who might be encouraged by your story of how Jesus has changed you: _____.

My prayer to God today is:

_____

_____

_____

_____

_____

_____

_____

_____

MICRO STUDY 4

Read 2 Corinthians 5:18–19.

Write out verse 19 here:

_____

_____

_____

_____

_____

It's important to note that God, through Christ, has restored the relationship between humans and himself. However, we have the privilege and duty of representing him to others. He did the work, but we get to be part of his ministry. How do you feel about being Jesus's representative?

If someone hasn't seen you in a while, what do you think they would notice has changed the most about you?

How have you changed since asking God to direct your thoughts, decisions, words, and actions?

Since we represent Jesus to others who haven't yet had a restart, why is it even more important to know Jesus intimately ourselves?

reconcile

Verb: to restore to friendship, compatibility, or harmony.*

reconciliation

Noun: an instance or occasion of friendly relations being restored.†

---

* *Merriam-Webster's Unabridged Dictionary*, s.v. "reconcile," accessed October 5, 2022, unabridged. merriam-webster.com/unabridged/ reconcile.

† Catherine Soanes and Angus Stevenson, eds., *Concise Oxford English Dictionary* (Oxford: Oxford University Press, 2004), accessed via Logos.

What do you think gets in the way of giving God full control of your life?

My prayer to God today is:

_____

_____

_____

_____

_____

_____

_____

_____

_____

MICRO STUDY 5

Read 2 Corinthians 5:20–21.

Write out verse 21 here:

_____

_____

_____

_____

_____

What does an ambassador to another country do?

Paul says God makes his appeal through the apostles. They speak for Christ when asking people to come back to God. They are his messengers, and so are we!

When you make a decision about something, how does word of mouth from a friend influence your decision?

Why is word of mouth powerful when it comes to people finding Jesus too?

Although our English Bibles use the noun *ambassadors*, it is actually a verb that is used in verse 20, meaning "to act as an ambassador or diplomat."* This isn't a title but an active role.

Ambassador isn't a fancy title. It isn't something we put on a bumper sticker. It's an assignment. What is the difference between a title and an assignment?

* Paul Barnett, *The Message of 2 Corinthians: Power in Weakness, The Bible Speaks Today* (Leicester, England; Downers Grove, IL: Inter-Varsity Press, 1988), 121.

How does focusing on a title lead to *entitlement* rather than a purpose?

Pause to meditate on this paraphrased version of verse 21 and put your name in the blank.

> For God made the sinless Christ to be the offering for
> _____'s sin, so that _____ could be
> made right with God through Christ.

My prayer to God today is:

_____

_____

_____

_____

_____

_____

_____

_____

Hope in Action

FIND A SMALL STACK OF STICKY NOTES. You may have to dig through the junk drawer, but you probably have some somewhere! If not, just cut a few three-inch squares from any paper and use tape. Any color will do.

In the spots below, write a word in each box that represents who you were before Jesus transformed your heart and mind—your old identity. Then begin covering each spot with a sticky note from your stack. On it, write a word or phrase that represents your new identity because of Jesus. You can add doodles or stickers or anything you'd like to jazz up the notes.

WEEK FOUR
REVIVE

Your lives are a letter written in our hearts
. . . a letter from Christ showing the result
of our ministry among you. . . . written
not with pen and ink, but with the Spirit
of the living God. It is carved not on
tablets of stone, but on human hearts.
—2 Corinthians 3:2–3

First Thoughts

IF YOU COULD GO BACK AND WRITE a letter to your teenage self, your twenty-something self, or even your five-years-ago self, what would you say?

Who was there to support you then?

What encouragement would have helped you to see life from a different perspective that may have been handy to understand sooner? Write what you wish someone had said to you.

_____

_____

_____

_____

_____

_____

_____

_____

_____

_____

_____

_____

_____

_____

_____

_____

_____

_____

_____

STORY

LAST WEEK, WE STUDIED WHAT IT MEANS to be given a new purpose. It's so important to know you don't have to live life alone! Living with purpose can be a challenge, and we need the love and support of other people. Sometimes that comes in a phone call or a conversation over coffee, and other times in a smile, a hug, or a pat on the shoulder.

When that encouragement comes in writing, it's so meaningful. It can be a note carried in your pocket or a letter saved between the pages of your Bible. It might be something you post on the refrigerator to view often.

When I was a teenager, the church I attended had these little yellow cards in the pews tucked in with the offering envelopes and stubby pencils like the ones used for mini golf. The yellow cards were there to promote writing encouragement notes to others in the church. More than once, one of these lifted my spirit when someone older and wiser wrote a Bible verse and some inspiration and handed that to me.

Decades past those teen years, I was sorting through several boxes of mementos. My husband and I dated as teens—met at church—and the box contained a mix of our memories. I pulled out one of those yellow cards. It was addressed to my husband, Phil, from our pastor's wife.

She'd written it around the time he graduated from high school and was trying to figure out what he wanted to do with his life, a really difficult time for him. It said:

> Have you ever considered full-time Christian ministry? I feel that God has gifted you with a tender heart and a loving spirit. God asks us to be plain ordinary earthen vessels into which he can pour the fullness of his power. I can see you in a youth pastor role or missionary or other role where you could touch lives for God. I'm praying for you.

If only Beth could have known. She left this earth long before God called Phil into ministry. He hates public speaking and sitting in a classroom, so her note made no logical sense at that time. That is, if you think inside the box. But God had a ministry in mind that we had never imagined—one that would blend Phil's heart for Jesus with his handyman skills and people skills. He's been in full-time ministry as a maintenance director at a Christian camp for seventeen years now.

Words of encouragement plant seeds that might take time to grow. But never underestimate the power of words.

LETTERS OF HOPE

Think back to when we didn't have email, computers, texting, social media, or the internet. I know. That might have been before your lifetime! Go back even more to when we couldn't leap across time zones by airplane and see our loved ones with instant travel. Think of the stories your grandparents and ancestors told. How did they communicate?

Written letters.

You may have written letters to someone when you were younger—perhaps to a grandparent under pressure from a parent to express thanks for a gift. I doubt you wrote as many as your ancestors did. Some of our grandparents built their entire courtship on letters. Mine did. My grandma and grandpa met before he shipped out in World War II, and they spent several years writing almost daily letters as he moved from country to country during the war. They planned out their whole life, scrawled in cursive on airmail stationery. I'm privileged to have those letters now.

Mail was a lifeline for soldiers. "For members of the armed forces the importance of mail during World War II was second only to food," according to an article from the Smithsonian National Postal Museum. "The emotional power of letters was heightened by the fear of loss and the need for communication during times of separation. . . . Emotions and feelings that were normally only expressed on special occasions were written regularly to ensure devotion and support."* Letters kept relationships going, and even allowed soldiers to kindle new relationships.

---

* "Victory Mail: Letter Writing in WWII," Smithsonian National Postal Museum (website), retrieved October 5, 2022, https://postalmuseum.si.edu/exhibition/victory-mail/letter-writing-in-wwii.

Ask a teenager now if they can fathom the idea of communication that took weeks to get a reply. It's hard to imagine checking the mailbox daily instead of checking a cell phone every few seconds.

ANCIENT LETTERS

This week, we're going to get an inside glimpse into some mail from long ago that we can still find encouraging today. Just as letters were a lifeline to soldiers in wartimes of the past, the apostle Paul's letters were a lifeline to the new Christian churches that were scattered around the Mediterranean and Aegean Seas.

These letters contained encouragement for members of the early New Testament church who needed to understand how to live as people remade into the image of Christ. As they grew and learned, they were reshaped to reflect the character and quality of Jesus.

The apostle Paul turned his transformation into determination to bring the good news of new life in Jesus Christ to people who had never heard truth before. After traveling around as a missionary of the gospel, he continued to write letters to the leaders of the churches he had visited. One-third of the New Testament contains letters, also called epistles, written by Paul. Imagine opening a letter delivered from one of Paul's couriers. Those words would revive the Christians and give them fresh courage to keep on. They could also correct and redirect.

Just as we still find encouragement and common ground in old correspondence from our ancestors, there is so much we can learn from Paul's letters. Yes, they were written to someone else, but they are still relevant to how the truth applies to us today.

Many contained warnings for the churches, and others contained instructions for how to live. Paul's tone and approach are also relevant leadership lessons for us to follow.

IS THERE A REASON?

When Paul experienced a dramatic interruption, it radically changed his purpose. He said, "But my life is worth nothing to me unless I use it for finishing the work assigned me by the Lord Jesus—the work

of telling others the Good News about the wonderful grace of God" (Acts 20:24).

It became his driving force in life. He had no fear. If he was living for the purpose God gave him, he didn't care what else happened. We have his letters to help us as we live out the purpose God has for our lives too.

When God "repurposes," he expects us to step into his mission for us. But what does this mean? Maybe you have heard someone say, "God has a purpose for everything," or, "Everything happens for a reason." If you're in the middle of a dark season where you'd give anything to have a glimpse of hope, these aren't encouraging words. Perhaps you aren't looking for a reason or a purpose right now but an escape door!

That's understandable.

There isn't any comfort in a flippant statement about a reason or a purpose for our difficulty. We absolutely acknowledge that there are experiences that are horrific, and no human should have to walk through them. We can't answer questions about why God allows suffering. He certainly doesn't *cause* it. But life also isn't meaningless. It's precious. God *has* to have a blueprint that surpasses the junk we experience.

And that's where hope can be revived.

Your pain isn't wasted. Your story isn't without meaning. God placed you on this earth to glorify him, and how that unfolds in each of our lives is different. Some will bring him glory by ministering to broken people. Others will come to that place through their own journey through brokenness. They will turn their heartbreak into an opportunity to walk others through similar pain.

Some will never know the reason for their struggle while here on earth, and they might never know how their example will touch the life of someone else. But God knows how your story becomes someone else's story—and how his purpose becomes your purpose. A repurposed life is one that has a new resolve, a new commitment, and a new determination to fulfill God's purpose above our own desires. It means being fully dedicated to walking with God—wherever that uncertain road leads.

PRAYER

GOD, WE WANT TO BE A GOOD representation of you and your love to the people we meet. We ask you to shape us into followers who resemble you in how we act and speak to the people in our lives. Teach us to be willing to accept our weaknesses as opportunities to display your power. Revive our courage. Help us trust your plan when it doesn't seem to have any purpose. We know you are more powerful than anything and able to work out our troubles for good. Amen.

EXPLORE THE WORD

FOLLOWING CHRIST DOESN'T MEAN WE WILL HAVE it easy. Some of our struggles come from things that fall within our control. But many are outside of our control. We might assume that once Jesus changes us, we will never wrestle with a desire to return to old behaviors. And if we do experience a struggle with being tempted by something from our past, we might see it as a hopeless place where we just slip back into our old character.

If you're feeling the angst from the back and forth between what you know God wants and your reality, are you ready for revival? In his letter to the Romans, Paul showed that he didn't give up. Like Paul, we keep on going when the struggle is real.

> I don't really understand myself, for I want to do what is right, but I don't do it. Instead, I do what I hate. But if I know that what I am doing is wrong, this shows that I agree that the law is good. So I am not the one doing wrong; it is sin living in me that does it.
>
> And I know that nothing good lives in me, that is, in my sinful nature. I want to do what is right, but I can't. I want to do what is good, but I don't. I don't want to do what is wrong, but I do it anyway. But if I do what I don't want to do, I am not really the one doing wrong; it is sin living in me that does it.

I have discovered this principle of life—that when I want to do what is right, I inevitably do what is wrong. I love God's law with all my heart. But there is another power within me that is at war with my mind. This power makes me a slave to the sin that is still within me. Oh, what a miserable person I am! Who will free me from this life that is dominated by sin and death? Thank God! The answer is in Jesus Christ our Lord. So you see how it is: In my mind I really want to obey God's law, but because of my sinful nature I am a slave to sin. (Romans 7:15–25)

In what way can you relate to Paul's struggle? What do you keep going back to even though you love Jesus?

What lies have you told yourself because of your struggle?

Wait! That wasn't the end of the story. Paul continued his letter in the next chapter with these words of hope: "So now there is no condemnation for those who belong to Christ Jesus. And because you belong to him, the power of the life-giving Spirit has freed you from the power of sin that leads to death" (Romans 8:1–2).

There has never been better news.

So, there is no judgment. Therefore, there is no disapproval. Thus, there is no sentence. Whichever way you express it, Jesus has made us free from keeping the law and following man-made, add-on rules to earn God's favor.

Describe what it means to you to be free from being condemned by rules and legalism.

> Therefore, dear brothers and sisters, you have no obliga-tion to do what your sinful nature urges you to do. For if you live by its dictates, you will die. But if through the power of the Spirit you put to death the deeds of your sinful nature, you will live. For all who are led by the Spirit of God are children of God.
>
> So you have not received a spirit that makes you fearful slaves. Instead, you received God's Spirit when he adopted you as his own children. Now we call him, "Abba, Father." (Romans 8:12–15)

Whew! Right? We are not condemned when we belong to Jesus. And because Jesus broke the bonds of sin, we can have victory too! We don't have to live in fear or defeat. More importantly, we are not obligated to be slaves to our human desires. The Holy Spirit gives us power for revival—if we put to death our sinful desires, we will have life!

Are we perfect? No. But God looks at our imperfections through a filter, as if Jesus himself stands between us and God the Father, and Jesus's own purity wipes out our blemishes. But if we keep our focus on our own imperfections and take our eyes off Jesus, we slide right back into victim mode and forget that Jesus has already won the vic-tory in the battle between good and evil.

> If we keep our focus on our own imperfections and take our eyes off Jesus, we slide right back into victim mode and forget that Jesus has already won the victory.

What are your thoughts when you hear this news?

Perhaps you need more assurance. Paul said more. Nothing can separate us from the love we have in Christ Jesus. He wrote, "Can anything ever separate us from Christ's love? Does it mean he no longer loves us if we have trouble or calamity, or are persecuted, or hungry, or destitute, or in danger, or threatened with death? . . . No, despite all these things, overwhelming victory is ours through Christ, who loved us" (Romans 8:35, 37).

Have you ever felt that way—as if the trouble you're going through must surely indicate God has turned his back on you and no longer loves you?

Notice how Paul mentioned both God's love and victory in this section. God triumphs over all suffering and every hostile power! I love how this commentary explains it: "Our security is in our relationship to Christ or in His relationship to us. The only harm that can come to us must first destroy this relationship. And the consolation here is that we are not holding Him. He is holding us. We are only yielding and responding. His love for us enables and inspires our love for Him. So we can confidently trust and rejoice in triumph."*

Think about a before-and-after project. Imagine you purchased a dresser from a thrift sale for five dollars, and you took it home. It

---

* Wilber T. Dayton, "The Epistle of Paul to the Romans," in Romans-Philemon, vol. 5, *The Wesleyan Bible Commentary* (Grand Rapids, MI: William B. Eerdmans Publishing Company, 1966), 59.

smelled like a combo of mildew and mothballs, had chips in the finish, and was missing some of the hardware. You fixed it up with new paint, fresh drawer lining, and new drawer pulls. It's as if you gave it a brand-new outfit.

Once the piece is transformed, it doesn't go back to the way it once was.

Who knew this better than Paul? After his radical change, he experienced suffering, persecution, death threats, legal troubles, physical struggles, and more. But he knew he had abundant power from the Spirit for whatever he faced—we do too. This includes our struggles with thoughts and attitudes.

In his letter to the church in Ephesus, Paul wrote about this.

> But that isn't what you learned about Christ. Since you have heard about Jesus and have learned the truth that comes from him, throw off your old sinful nature and your former way of life, which is corrupted by lust and deception. Instead, let the Spirit renew your thoughts and attitudes. Put on your new nature, created to be like God—truly righteous and holy. (Ephesians 4:20–24)

This is what it means to be renewed. The new way takes on the life and the character of Christ. It isn't learning *about* Jesus but becoming *like* him. Revival is new life, a rejection of the old and receiving a brand-new nature. That's why there's an "instead" in the passage. It isn't a both/and situation. We can't keep our old way of life and be renewed in our thoughts and attitudes.

> Revival is new life, a rejection of the old and receiving a brand-new nature.

How would you describe the difference between knowing about Jesus and being truly renewed?

Which holdover thoughts and attitudes from your old nature are you ready to surrender for transformation?

NO GOING BACK

There is no going back. Imagine if Paul went back to persecuting Christians every time he had a discouraging day. Being remade and renewed, repurposed, and revived is a process forward. We throw off our old nature like a sweatshirt covered in vomit. Ick. We wouldn't put it back on again!

> In a moment of weakness, it's easy to doubt what God can do.

We're to put on a new nature—fresh clothing! Paul said this same thing in a letter to the church at Colossae: "Put on your new nature, and be renewed as you learn to know your Creator and become like him. In this new life, it doesn't matter if you are a Jew or a Gentile, circumcised or uncircumcised, barbaric, uncivilized, slave, or free. Christ is all that matters, and he lives in all of us" (Colossians 3:10–11).

In a moment of weakness, it's easy to doubt what God can do. But when we feel the weakest, that's when God is the most powerful. That's why our purpose is to bring glory to him. Our before-and-after story should point people to God in such a way that they can say, "Isn't God amazing? If you knew her before, you would understand the dramatic transformation she has been through."

AN IRRITATING THORN

Paul had something he referred to as a thorn in the flesh. This wasn't a literal thorn but something just as irritating as one, and we're never told what it was. Think of how it feels when you have a sliver in your skin. It can drive you crazy until you get it out! He had begged God to remove this "thorn," but God didn't. And then in a letter to the Christians in Corinth, Paul provided insight about the purpose God may have had for giving him a no answer every time he asked for deliverance from this thing.

> Each time he said, "My grace is all you need. My power works best in weakness." So now I am glad to boast about my weaknesses, so that the power of Christ can work through me. That's why I take pleasure in my weaknesses, and in the insults, hardships, persecutions, and troubles that I suffer for Christ. For when I am weak, then I am strong. (2 Corinthians 12:9–10)

Could it be as simple as that? Could it be that sometimes the purpose for our most irritating things is for us to keep our focus centered on God? To keep us humble enough to remember we can't do this life on our own? To remind us that we have been remade by the Creator, the one who knew our purpose from the beginning, and he has a plan for our lives?

What does it mean to "take pleasure" in the struggle?

Sometimes it seems as if living for Jesus is so upside down. When I am weak, then I am strong. I boast about my weakness, not my power. I become a slave to Christ so that I can experience freedom. We humble ourselves so God can lift us up. Our trials can produce beauty.

The upside-down way doesn't give clear answers to the questions: Why me? Why now? What are you doing, God? When will this end? But it gives enough hope to keep us pressing on.

LETTER OF RECOMMENDATION

There is one other type of letter we haven't discussed—a letter of recommendation. If you have ever written one, you know it's written on behalf of another person, explaining their credentials and endorsing their skills or character.

> The only letter of recommendation we need is you yourselves. Your lives are a letter written in our hearts; everyone can read it and recognize our good work among you. Clearly, you are a letter from Christ showing the result of our ministry among you. This "letter" is written not with pen and ink, but with the Spirit of the living God. It is carved not on tablets of stone, but on human hearts. (2 Corinthians 3:2–3)

Here, Paul said he didn't need a letter of recommendation written about his ministry to validate it. Instead, his ministry is validated by the lives of those who have been changed by the gospel. Ultimately, they are all living letters representing Jesus Christ since the gospel is Paul's ministry.

The human letters I have in my box of mementos fade. They're yellowed, and the paper is fragile. But a changed life is a letter that doesn't fall apart.

How we choose to live becomes a letter that can be read by everyone we meet. Our behavior is evidence of true transformation. Our real story isn't written on paper but shown on our faces and in our actions, carried in the tone of our words, and read through the love we show. That says more than words could ever say.

Which part of your "letter," your personal story, tells others about the power of Jesus?

> Our real story isn't written on paper but shown on our faces and in our actions, carried in the tone of our words, and read through the love we show.

Remember how proud Paul was of his Jewish heritage? He had done all the religious things that were part of the ritual of being a "good person," but that pursuit had led him down the wrong road. In his letter to the Christians at Philippi, he explained how religiosity and tradition meant nothing in the grand picture. "I once thought these things were valuable, but now I consider them worthless because of what Christ has done. Yes, everything else is worthless when compared with the infinite value of knowing Christ Jesus my Lord. For his sake I have discarded everything else, counting it all as garbage, so that I could gain Christ" (Philippians 3:7–8).

> No amount of religious tradition or attempts to be a good person, or memorizing the ten commandments, or being confirmed or baptized, or going to church every week will take care of our sin problem.

No amount of religious tradition or attempts to be a good person, or memorizing the ten commandments, or being confirmed or baptized, or going to church every week will take care of our sin problem. Only Jesus's sacrifice paid the price that would renew us—paid the death penalty for us—so we can experience new life in him.

All those good things are nothing but garbage if we try to use them to substitute for real transformation. And real transformation demonstrates evidence of our great God—a testimony of his power.

What letter do you want the next generation to "read" from your life?

If you could sum it up in one word, what would that be?

Prayer Journal

I'M THANKFUL FOR:

_____

_____

_____

_____

_____

_____

I'M ASKING GOD FOR:

_____

_____

_____

_____

_____

WORDS OF WORSHIP TO GOD:

_____

_____

_____

_____

_____

_____

APPLY

MICRO STUDY 1

Read Colossians 3:1–4.

Write out verses 2–3 here:

_____

_____

_____

_____

_____

_____

_____

_____

_____

_____

What is our "why," according to this passage?

Why should we be motivated to think about heavenly things instead of only ourselves?

Paul had a radical outlook on his life. It wasn't worth anything unless the gospel went forward. He said, "But my life is worth nothing to me unless I use it for finishing the work assigned me by the Lord

Jesus—the work of telling others the Good News about the wonderful grace of God" (Acts 20:24).

Think about the things that matter to you. What would it be like if you could fill in the blank with the priorities, activities, possessions, dreams, and goals to make a statement like that. Try it. Fill in the blank below and think about how hard it is to put your passions there:

> But _____ is worth nothing to me unless
> I use it for finishing the work assigned me by the Lord
> Jesus—the work of telling others the Good News about
> the wonderful grace of God.

What is the most difficult thing for you to put in that blank?

My prayer to God today is:

_____

_____

_____

_____

_____

_____

_____

_____

_____

_____

MICRO STUDY 2

Read Colossians 3:5–9.

Write out verses 7–8 here:

_____

_____

_____

_____

_____

_____

_____

_____

_____

_____

What are the character traits that don't belong anymore when we follow Christ?

When you see phrases such as "used to do" and "stripped off your old sinful nature" (in the NLT), how does this indicate more than just good intentions?

As you think about how you use social media, how you treat people in the checkout line and interact with the people at home and out in the community, how does your "letter" read?

What would you like to change about it, beginning now?

Read 2 Timothy 3:14–17. Paul's written letters were meant to encourage people, instruct them on how to live, and rebuke anything that was off-base in their lives. In what way is *all* of Scripture actually a letter for us?

My prayer to God today is:

_____

_____

_____

_____

_____

_____

_____

MICRO STUDY 3

Read Colossians 3:10–12.

Write out verse 12 here:

_____

_____

_____

_____

_____

_____

_____

These verses talk about renewal, not only in spiritual knowledge but in conduct too. What does it say about really knowing your Creator?

What distinctions do you notice in Christian churches that would be similar to the New Testament divisions Paul listed in this passage?

What happens when Christians forget that *Christ* binds them together?

Your past died with Christ in his death because he died to break the bondage. The person you once were no longer exists. You took off that old identity like dirty clothes. Your new identity is in Jesus. Our fallen world divides by race, culture, status, social position, and influence. But the overarching identity as **one** group of people in Jesus crushes these divisions.

How does it make you feel knowing God doesn't have favorites?

Which of the qualities in verse 12 would you like God to work on in you?

My prayer to God today is:

_____

_____

_____

_____

_____

_____

_____

_____

_____

_____

_____

MICRO STUDY 4

Read Colossians 3:13–15.

Write out verses 14–15 here:

_____

_____

_____

_____

_____

_____

_____

_____

_____

_____

What did it mean when Paul said to make allowance for one another's faults?

How is making allowance for someone's faults not the same as excusing abusive behavior?

We need to look at the whole of Scripture when considering what God says about forgiveness. I want to give the disclaimer that too often, people overlook blatant and intentional spiritual, emotional, and physical abuse because someone else has misapplied this passage. Forgiving is not the same as keeping silent or letting someone off the hook for intentional behavior.

Pastor Tony Evans described forgiveness this way, "Forgiveness does *not* mean approving a sin or excusing evil. Rather, forgiveness means releasing people from obligations incurred by their wrongs against you. This may come in the form of unilateral forgiveness— that is, forgiving someone who has not asked for forgiveness. Or it may come in the form of transactional forgiveness, which involves the confession of the offender, his repentance, and reconciliation. What makes forgiveness possible is recognizing that **the Lord has forgiven you**."*

What is the basis for how we treat others, according to Colossians 3:13?

---

* *CSB Tony Evans Study Bible*, (Nashville: Holman Bible Publishers, 2017), note on Colossians 3:13, as found on BibleGateway.com.

Why do you think love is the thing that tops everything? How does it affect the other qualities?

Who is God challenging you to love and forgive?

How is unforgiveness hindering your peace and your effectiveness as a Christian right now?

My prayer to God today is:

_____

_____

_____

_____

_____

_____

_____

_____

_____

MICRO STUDY 5

Read Colossians 3:16–17.

Write out verse 17 here:

_____

_____

_____

_____

_____

_____

What is the main message of our lives according to verse 16?

What does it look like to have the message about Christ (the word of Christ in other translations) fill your life?

What is God nudging you to change about your current practices?

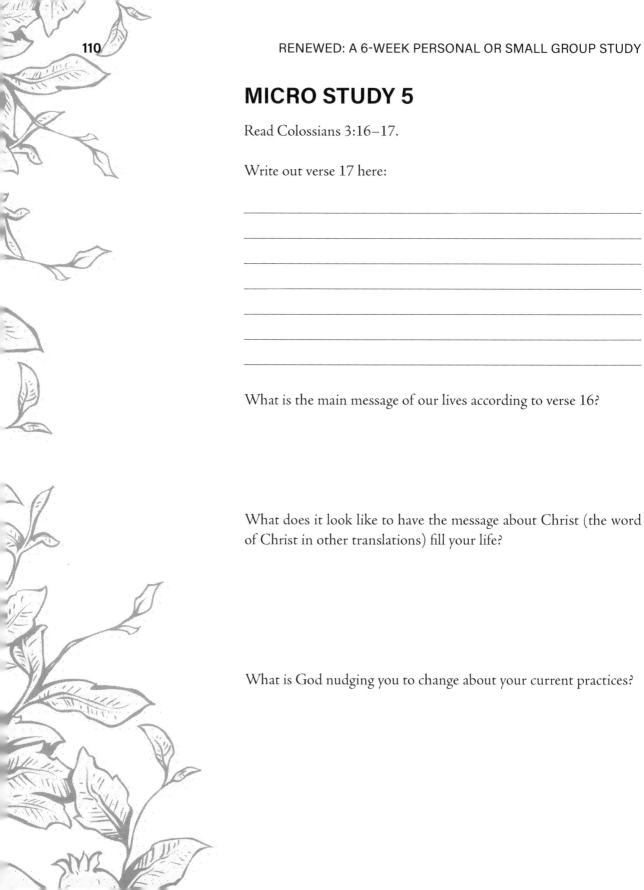

Why is thanksgiving (thankful hearts) an important factor as we live with other Christians, teaching and warning one another?

How is our conduct all tied together in worship, work, recreation, and relationships? Why do you think it says it applies to whatever you do?

How does worship with other Christians revive you?

My prayer to God today is:

_____

_____

_____

_____

_____

_____

_____

_____

_____

Hope in Action

MAKE A HABIT OF ENCOURAGING OTHERS WITH handwritten notes. Keep a few note cards in your Bible, on the kitchen table, in a basket by the coffee pot (writing while you wait), or in your purse. Fill out a card any time the Holy Spirit brings someone to your mind. You could write a note when you do your morning devotions or while you're waiting for an appointment. Think of all the instances where you naturally pick up your phone to pass the time.

Who can you encourage right now? Pause to write a note and send it off.

WEEK FIVE
REJOICE

*I will be filled with joy because of you. I will
sing praises to your name, O Most High.*
—Psalm 9:2

First Thoughts

MAKE A LIST OF WHAT FILLS YOUR heart with gratitude and brings you joy just thinking about it.

_____

_____

_____

_____

_____

_____

_____

_____

_____

_____

_____

_____

_____

_____

_____

_____

_____

_____

_____

_____

_____

STORY

MOUNDED BUCKETS AND BOXES OF APPLES OBSTRUCTED the path to the kitchen sink. Rows of empty jars stood at attention on the counter, and dozens of quarts of blush-colored applesauce cooled on the table. I was up to my elbows in apples and sauce. While prepared fruit bubbled on the stove, I continued grabbing and cutting washed apples from the sink. On another burner, the canner simmered with jars of hot applesauce.

When my children were small, they would vie for turns cranking the cooked apples through the sauce strainer. Now, it was my solo job. All that time standing in the kitchen gave me plenty of time to think. I wasn't yet into podcasts or audiobooks. It was just me and the radio and a million thoughts.

I chose a perfect apple—a beautiful red one without a mar on the outside—and thought it would be nice if they were all like that. However, when I sliced into it, the knife revealed a black core with a little worm wiggling inside. *Eew!* I dropped it as if it were scalding me. I swear that creature was grinning at me. *Gotcha*!

What a reminder of how life can be. We can fake an attitude for just so long until something reveals what's really going on inside. Bitterness can rot our joy and eat us up from the inside out—like that nasty little worm in the apple—and someone eventually discovers it.

Conversely, I noted that not every apple that is marred on the outside is ugly on the inside. Sometimes, my apples can have so many scabs that I'm tempted to toss them straight into the compost bucket without peeling or cutting into them. However, the inside flesh is often perfectly crisp and white.

Looking at the outside of someone's life doesn't always tell us about what's going on in their heart either. Some of the people with the heaviest hardships are the most joyful people. Challenges and disappointments have a way of revealing the heart. I admire people who respond to each new difficulty with unexpected peace.

BOILING AND TESTING

Without heating apples, there is no sauce. When I put them on the stove and turn up the heat, that's when the aroma fills the kitchen.

That's when the sweetness oozes from the fruit. When I press it through the crank strainer, the smooth, delicious sauce seeps into a serving bowl, and the peelings and core come out the other end into a pile that I toss into the compost bin.

When God transforms a life, he often turns up the heat to turn us into something that pleases him. My fresh apples will last for only a short time before turning brown and rotting. But I can preserve the fruit for a long time by cooking them and canning the sauce.

When we go through situations that test our faith, it's often difficult for us to see God's bigger and better plan, but the joy that comes from trusting him is sweeter and longer lasting than any temporary happiness that we can experience with our own efforts.

Applesauce reminds me that some parts must be discarded. There are some things God needs to dispose of when he works on us. When God allows our faith to be tested through trials, we're in a good place for him to begin to work on our character. When God helps us discard things such as pride, jealousy, self-centeredness, and greed, he softens our hearts and makes us more like Jesus.

The apostle Paul knew what it was like to be tested. To be pressed. To experience the heat of court trials and imprisonment. Despite it all, he often talked about rejoicing.

PRAYER

HEAVENLY FATHER, MAY WE ALWAYS BE FILLED with the fruit of our salvation—the righteous character produced in our lives by Jesus Christ. We want to bring much glory and praise to you, God, as you re-create us in your image. Help us to understand true joy and to rejoice in whatever circumstances life brings. Amen.

EXPLORE THE WORD

BEING RENEWED INCLUDES BEING REDEEMED, HAVING A restart, being repurposed, and experiencing a revival. That leads to an overwhelming sense of rejoicing! No, not the temporary fizzle I get when I pour my afternoon diet soda—no judgment, please. That fizz might bubble right out of the cup if I pour too fast, but then it's over. Instead, the kind of rejoicing I'm talking about is an underlying joy that's present through everything. An effervescence that never goes away.

> I pray that your love will overflow more and more, and that you will keep on growing in knowledge and understanding. For I want you to understand what really matters, so that you may live pure and blameless lives until the day of Christ's return. May you always be filled with the fruit of your salvation—the righteous character produced in your life by Jesus Christ—for this will bring much glory and praise to God. (Philippians 1:9–11)

Notice how Paul prayed first for overflowing love. Why is love the fountain of joy?

What is the fruit of salvation, according to Paul?

Paul wrote: "Whatever happens, my dear brothers and sisters, rejoice in the Lord. I never get tired of telling you these things, and I do it to safeguard your faith" (Philippians 3:1). *Whatever* happens!

There was a time when a health concern or even a *potential* diagnosis of a serious illness would send me seeking out all the what-ifs. When the internet came around, Dr. Google made it worse. Now I can research every symptom or possibility if I wish to. As a registered nurse, I already know enough to be dangerous, but with the interwebs, I can now find every risk *and* read testimonials from people who have experienced it.

Over time, God has given me less of a desire to know the what-ifs and fewer urges to plan for every possibility. Several years ago, God proved this peace was real when I went to the doctor for some perimenopausal symptoms that weren't "normal." Does perimenopause really have anything truly normal about it? An ultrasound showed that my uterus had decided it wasn't going to give up without one last overachieving fight. It was far beyond thicker than average and sporting a little growth of some sort.

While I waited for the procedure to remove this mysterious "thing" that turned out to be an unusual type of fibroid, God gave me peace about waiting until the procedure was over and getting the results in before I researched all the possibilities for this UFO (unidentified fibroid object, and yes, I made that up) in my uterus. He gave me calm peace that whatever happened, God would direct the next step.

When have you had to wait for results of some kind, and God gave you peace?

When didn't you have peace, and what did you learn through that?

What is your "whatever happens" situation right now?

I'm thankful that I didn't waste time with the worry and a lot of research. The procedure was successful in removing the UFO, and there was no evidence of cancer in the lining they removed.

Our "whatever happens" situations don't include all the things that they did for Paul and his cohorts in the New Testament. Persecution has a way of bringing some perspective to it all.

The other thing that brings perspective for me is that all the things we do for God are nothing in comparison to having true life. Paul described his spiritual heritage as a pure-blooded citizen of Israel and a Pharisee. And then he said this about that pedigree:

> I once thought these things were valuable, but now I consider them worthless because of what Christ has done. Yes, everything else is worthless when compared with the infinite value of knowing Christ Jesus my Lord.
>
> For his sake I have discarded everything else, counting it all as garbage, so that I could gain Christ and become one with him. I no longer count on my own righteousness through obeying the law; rather, I become righteous through faith in Christ. For God's way of making us right with himself depends on faith.
>
> I want to know Christ and experience the mighty power that raised him from the dead. I want to suffer with him, sharing in his death, so that one way or another I will experience the resurrection from the dead!
>
> I don't mean to say that I have already achieved these things or that I have already reached perfection. But I press on to possess that perfection for which Christ Jesus first possessed me. No, dear brothers and sisters, I have not achieved it, but I focus on this one thing: Forgetting the past and looking forward to what lies ahead, I press on to reach the end of the race and receive the heavenly prize for which God, through Christ Jesus, is calling us. (Philippians 3:7–14)

(chairō). vb. **rejoice, be glad.** *Be in a state of gladness, happiness, or well-being.* "The kind of rejoicing the term *chairō* denotes is not only a feeling and expression of joy but also an action one chooses."[*]

---

[*] Kenneth D. Litwak, "Joy," in *Lexham Theological Wordbook*, ed. Douglas Mangum et al., Lexham Bible Reference Series (Bellingham, WA: Lexham Press, 2014).

Paul chose to forget the past and look ahead because it was so much more than what had already changed in him. This is why he rejoiced.

He had been changed, but he had not arrived. And God had something wonderful prepared for the future.

Rejoicing implies gratitude for what God has done. What work has he done in you that you are grateful for?

What part of your spiritual "pedigree" is worth nothing in comparison with what it means to truly follow Jesus?

What rules, or "law," have you tried to follow to somehow prove yourself as righteous to others?

When Paul talked about wanting to share in Christ's death, it was the same type of language he used in other letters. He was talking about a daily death to self and our own desires in exchange for Jesus's mindset. Some writers have referred to this as cruciformity (being conformed to the cross) or Christiformity (being conformed to Christ). I've heard these terms in books and podcasts. But what do they mean?

It is being changed inside and out to be like Jesus.

Remember the applesauce illustration? When we're really heated and pressed, that's when we find out how much like Jesus we are.

What situation presses your buttons and brings out words and actions you aren't proud of?

I've discovered mine is fear. Feeling out of control or fearing the unknown can produce a meltdown, targeting my husband as I overreact in anger. But listen to how Paul explained being conformed to Jesus's attitudes and mindset.

> Is there any encouragement from belonging to Christ? Any comfort from his love? Any fellowship together in the Spirit? Are your hearts tender and compassionate? Then make me truly happy by agreeing wholeheartedly with each other, loving one another, and working together with one mind and purpose.
>
> Don't be selfish; don't try to impress others. Be humble, thinking of others as better than yourselves. Don't look out only for your own interests, but take an interest in others, too. You must have the same attitude that Christ Jesus had.
>
> Though he was God, he did not think of equality with God as something to cling to. Instead, he gave up his divine privileges; he took the humble position of a slave and was born as a human being. When he appeared in human form, he humbled himself in obedience to God and died a criminal's death on a cross. (Philippians 2:1–8)

Pause for a moment and reflect. What does it mean to you to know Jesus exchanged his divine privilege to become a slave and die?

When Paul wrote to the Philippians, he was imprisoned in Rome.

> Always be full of joy in the Lord. I say it again—rejoice! Let everyone see that you are considerate in all you do. Remember, the Lord is coming soon.
>
> Don't worry about anything; instead, pray about everything. Tell God what you need, and thank him for all he has done. Then you will experience God's peace, which exceeds anything we can understand. His peace will guard your hearts and minds as you live in Christ Jesus.
>
> And now, dear brothers and sisters, one final thing. Fix your thoughts on what is true, and honorable, and right, and pure, and lovely, and admirable. Think about things that are excellent and worthy of praise. Keep putting into practice all you learned and received from me—everything you heard from me and saw me doing. Then the God of peace will be with you. (Philippians 4:4–9)

Briefly summarize Paul's words from Philippians 4 above in your own words as a manifesto on how to live a joyful life.

The noun "joy" (*charis*) occurred seven times in the short letter to the Philippians. The verb "rejoice" occurred eight times. That makes fifteen times he said something stemming from a word for joy. *

* George A. Turner, "The Epistle of Paul to the Philippians," in *Romans-Philemon*, vol. 5, *The Wesleyan Bible Commentary* (Grand Rapids, MI: William B. Eerdmans Publishing Company, 1966), 476.

My prayer of blessing for you comes from Paul's words: "And this same God who takes care of me will supply all your needs from his glorious riches, which have been given to us in Christ Jesus. Now all glory to God our Father forever and ever! Amen" (Philippians 4:19–20).

Finish this statement based on Philippians 3:13. Forgetting the past and focusing on God's wonderful future for me, I rejoice because:

_____

_____

_____

_____

_____

_____

Prayer Journal

I'M THANKFUL FOR:

_____

_____

_____

_____

_____

_____

I'M ASKING GOD FOR:

_____

_____

_____

_____

_____

_____

WORDS OF WORSHIP TO GOD:

_____

_____

_____

_____

_____

_____

APPLY

MICRO STUDY 1

Write out 1 Thessalonians 5:16–18 here:

_____

_____

_____

_____

_____

_____

_____

_____

Paul said to always be joyful. Obviously, this isn't something we fake for show. What kind of underlying joy do you think Paul was describing?

In Philippians 4:4, Paul expanded on this and said to always be full of joy in the Lord. How is that different than rejoicing in our circumstances?

In Ephesians 6:18, Paul said to "pray in the Spirit at all times and on every occasion." If you were brought up only with formal prayers in church, this might be something uncomfortable at first. However, you can have conversations with God in your head or out loud at any time. I'm that person who looks as if she's talking to herself while driving. God is often my invisible passenger.

These can be short prayers. Or long. You can talk to God throughout the day. Paul paired that with being thankful at all times.

What might your typical day be like if you started to rejoice always, pray continually, and give thanks for everything?

How might it change your mindset?

My prayer to God today is:

_____

_____

_____

_____

_____

_____

_____

_____

MICRO STUDY 2

Read Philippians 2:12–18.

Write out verses 14–15 here:

_____

_____

_____

_____

_____

_____

_____

_____

_____

_____

Complaining and arguing represent the opposite of joy. How do you feel when you grumble and complain?

How can the *absence* of arguing or complaining shine to others even more than our preaching?

How would you have felt if Paul had written this in a letter to you and used "lose my life" and "share that joy" all in the same thought?

What might you lose by wholeheartedly following Jesus right now? What might you gain?

What joy have you experienced in the past as you obeyed Jesus?

My prayer to God today is:

_____

_____

_____

_____

_____

_____

_____

_____

MICRO STUDY 3

Read Philippians 4:10–17.

Write out verse 12 here:

_____

_____

_____

_____

_____

_____

_____

Think of when you have experienced discontentment because you felt you were lacking something. How did it feel?

How can even having prosperity lead to discontentment?

What was Paul's secret for contentment?

Paul explained how other Christians met his needs. How does providing for others' needs bring you joy?

Paul described having moral support from other Christians. When have you felt joyful because of how someone loved and supported you in your emotional need?

My prayer to God today is:

_____

_____

_____

_____

_____

_____

_____

_____

MICRO STUDY 4

Read Romans 5:1–5.

Write out verse 3 here:

_____

_____

_____

_____

_____

_____

Paul told the Christians in Rome they could rejoice even when they ran into problems and trials. He included himself in the "we," which also includes us. Why can we rejoice?

Peace with God isn't just a feeling. It's a state of being. Describe the difference.

How does this peace lead to the ability to rejoice when problems come?

What is it that we are joyfully looking forward to, according to verse 2?

What problems or challenges have strengthened your endurance? How have they built your character?

What is your confident hope in the middle of everything you go through, whether good or bad?

My prayer to God today is:

_____

_____

_____

_____

_____

_____

_____

_____

_____

MICRO STUDY 5

Write out 2 Corinthians 13:11 here:

_____

_____

_____

_____

_____

_____

How do joy, spiritual growth and maturity, encouragement from others, and living in harmony and peace all contribute to a more satisfying life?

When you watch the news or scroll through social media, which of the above things do you find missing?

Perhaps you said all of them. You wouldn't be lying! Paul wasn't telling the Corinthians that they needed to all think the same. How can you live in harmony and peace with others when you think differently?

A spiritually mature person will respond differently than someone who is just starting out as a Christian. How have your responses changed from how you were when you first started following Jesus?

What has God challenged you to change this week as you studied what it means to rejoice?

My prayer to God today is:

_____

_____

_____

_____

_____

_____

_____

_____

Hope in Action

PAUL FOUND PEACE AND CONTENTMENT WHEN GOD gave him strength and his fellow Christians helped meet his emotional and physical needs. Who can you encourage? Here are some ideas:

- Bake something and share it with a friend or neighbor.
- Invite someone who is struggling to have coffee and let her pour her heart out.
- Pray for someone right there rather than saying, "I'll pray for you." Do it! On the phone, at the mall, typed out in a text message.
- Send a gift card to someone for groceries or even a splurge from their favorite boutique.
- Offer to watch a friend's children for a few hours.
- Send a care package.
- Offer to drive someone to a doctor's appointment.

WEEK SIX
REPEAT

But you must continue to believe this truth and stand firmly in it. Don't drift away from the assurance you received when you heard the Good News.
—Colossians 1:23

First Thoughts

WHAT WAS THE MOST SPECIAL DAY OF your life so far? What would you like to repeat about it if you could?

_____

_____

_____

_____

_____

_____

_____

_____

_____

_____

_____

_____

_____

_____

_____

_____

_____

_____

_____

STORY

A FRIEND TEXTED ME A PICTURE OF an ad about a free class at the fitness center. The description said, "This multiweek evidence-based strength training program is designed for middle-aged and older women and men. Each class includes progressive weight training, flexibility, and balance activities."

Did I mention the class was *free?* Twice a week at the gym for free. I don't really like group workouts, but this seemed doable, and I needed a fitness restart.

There were two options: regular and advanced.

I decided I should do the regular. After all, I had no idea what I was doing and had no business calling myself advanced in any fitness area.

But, as I thought about it more, I decided I should check to get more details. I emailed the program coordinator.

It turned out that the qualification for the advanced class was that I could get up off the floor without assistance. No Life Alert necklace needed here. So, I bumped up to the advanced class.

We gathered at 9:00 a.m. in the aerobics room of the fitness center. Others were already there with their hand weights and yoga mats. They were chatting as if they knew each other. I found a spot and glanced around the room.

It was fair to assume I was the youngest person in the class—by far.

We started our workout with slow-motion squats. The instructor reminded us that this exercise would build the muscles we needed to get up and down from a chair safely. She explained that plopping into a chair with a giant whoosh wasn't good for our bodies.

Oops.

Our slow-motion squats began from a seated position on a chair, and we slowly rose to the count of four, then slowly sat to the count of four.

The instructor started a 1950s song on the Bluetooth speaker, and we were off.

Up, two, three, four.

Down, two, three, four.

After a brief tap of the bottom on the chair, we started the next rep. Before the end of the second set of reps, granny fitness was already kicking my behind. Literally. I think I felt several exercises kick my patootie.

My right thigh trembled in fear of what I might do to it next. I'm not kidding. It actually trembled. I looked down as I stood on tippy toes for a thirty-second eternity, and I hadn't imagined it. The cuff of my yoga capris quivered. A lot.

We did wrist exercises to "help us with the dexterity to operate a can opener" and reaches to improve our coordination for getting things from the cupboard. Some exercises were to strengthen the muscles that would make us less fall prone.

When I arrived home, I could hardly lift my thighs high enough to ascend the stairs to my main living area. In fact, I almost tripped and fell. Which I found to be a little ironic, considering the purpose of the class, after all.

I moved around like someone who was eighty-eight instead of forty-eight for a few days before going back for more torture. Those grannies have some spunk!

A restart can be painful. But it can be beautiful. And a true restart comes with a repeat. The only way to improve is to go back and repeat the exercise.

The only way to maintain any sort of spiritual fitness after a restart is to repeat the steps and create habits. Then we reach true renewal.

PRAYER

LORD, THANK YOU FOR YOUR PATIENCE AS we practice being more like you. Thank you for giving us the desire and the power to be renewed. Show us how to do so even more. Amen.

EXPLORE THE WORD

PAUL SAID, "DEAR BROTHERS AND SISTERS, WE urge you in the name of the Lord Jesus to live in a way that pleases God, as we have taught you. You live this way already, and we encourage you to do so even more" (1 Thessalonians 4:1). When we've committed to following Christ, we go "back to the gym" over and over. We "do so even more" by strengthening and renewing our minds.

Jesus himself explained it to his disciples this way: "If any of you wants to be my follower, you must give up your own way, take up your cross daily, and follow me. If you try to hang on to your life, you will lose it. But if you give up your life for my sake, you will save it" (Luke 9:23–24).

Daily sounds like repeating, doesn't it? Christianity is not a one-and-done thing. Let me clarify that. Jesus died once for all. But our living as his followers requires daily practice.

To stay on this journey of renewal, we circle back and repeat habits, study God's Word, and practice living like Jesus until it sticks. If I try to learn a silly dance on TikTok, I have to watch a video on repeat. Frankly, it still doesn't stick. I'm not coordinated that way at all.

But it should come as no surprise that imitating Jesus takes observing him on repeat. Practicing until we understand how he moves and thinks. Paul wrote a letter to an evangelist and companion named Timothy.

> Now the Holy Spirit tells us clearly that in the last times some will turn away from the true faith; they will follow deceptive spirits and teachings that come from demons. These people are hypocrites and liars, and their consciences are dead.
>
> They will say it is wrong to be married and wrong to eat certain foods. But God created those foods to be eaten with thanks by faithful people who know the truth. Since everything God created is good, we should not reject any of it but receive it with thanks. For we know it is made acceptable by the word of God and prayer.

Timothy was a native of Lystra and a companion of Paul. A third-generation Christian. His name is the combination of two Greek words: *time*, meaning "honor, reverence," and *theos*, meaning "God." Timothy was the son of a Jewish woman and a Greek father (Acts 16:1–2).[*]

[*] Cliff Kvidahl, "Timothy," in *The Lexham Bible Dictionary*, ed. John D. Barry et al. (Bellingham, WA: Lexham Press, 2016).

If you explain these things to the brothers and sisters, Timothy, you will be a worthy servant of Christ Jesus, one who is nourished by the message of faith and the good teaching you have followed. Do not waste time arguing over godless ideas and old wives' tales. Instead, train yourself to be godly. "Physical training is good, but training for godliness is much better, promising benefits in this life and in the life to come." This is a trustworthy saying, and everyone should accept it. This is why we work hard and continue to struggle, for our hope is in the living God, who is the Savior of all people and particularly of all believers. (1 Timothy 4:1–10)

What was Paul writing about here? What was the concern?

What false "rules" and conditions have possibly distracted you from truly following God? (Think about political or social rules that might be falsely associated with being a Christian. Or rules about what you can listen to and watch.)

What are some examples of training for godliness?

In what way does "training" imply repetition?

Is there anything legalistic about your beliefs about spiritual practices (sometimes called spiritual disciplines)? For example, have you created specific rules for yourself about reading your Bible or praying that cause you to feel shame or guilt if you don't do them perfectly?

> *gymnazō* is a Greek verb used in 1 Timothy 4:7. It means "**to train, to undergo discipline.** It is literally to train for physical exercise, but it is also used figuratively of spiritual and mental exercise, which thus means to train or undergo discipline."[*]

---

* Michael Scott Robertson, "Discipline," in *Lexham Theological Wordbook*, ed. Douglas Mangum et al., Lexham Bible Reference Series (Bellingham, WA: Lexham Press, 2014).

If you could define the purpose of spiritual practices (disciplines), how would you summarize it in a sentence or two?

Even though spiritual training is important, and repetition leads to maturity, we need to be careful that we don't turn our habits into rules that miss the purpose of it all and become false doctrines of their own. I've heard people get worked up about the idea that a "quiet time" is mandated in the Bible. This is a phrase many Christians use to describe their time of daily private devotion and prayer.

However, the Christians in Paul's and Timothy's time didn't have gilded leather Bibles with daily meditations and devotions in the sidebar. I caution all of us against creating rules that are based on our own cultural interpretation rather than on the simple habits God established through his apostles.

Examples of habits, practices, and disciplines that some people "exercise" routinely. Note: there is no such thing as an official list.

Prayer

Worship

Bible study

Sabbath

Scripture memory

Confession

Meditation

Silence

Solitude

Retreat

Fasting

Service

Celebration

Frugality

Abstinence

Generosity

Fellowship

Teach these things and insist that everyone learn them. Don't let anyone think less of you because you are young. Be an example to all believers in what you say, in the way you live, in your love, your faith, and your purity. Until I get there, focus on reading the Scriptures to the church, encouraging the believers, and teaching them. (1 Timothy 4:11–13)

What examples of training did Paul give here?

When have you been timid because of your age, thinking you didn't have the wisdom and experience to influence others? (It might be now or in the past.)

Based on what Paul said to Timothy, what encouragement can you find here about serving wholeheartedly, no matter your age?

If you stop exercising your physical muscles, they weaken. What happens when we get lazy about our spiritual muscles? (Again, this is about your personal development and not about rules.)

When are you most vulnerable to discouragement and temptation? (Think about it both physically and spiritually.)

Paul wrote a letter to the church at Ephesus and talked about growing more mature. He also explained how Jesus has given all believers different tasks and roles:

> Now these are the gifts Christ gave to the church: the apostles, the prophets, the evangelists, and the pastors and teachers. Their responsibility is to equip God's people to do his work and build up the church, the body of Christ. This will continue until we all come to such unity in our faith and knowledge of God's Son that we will be mature in the Lord, measuring up to the full and complete standard of Christ.
>
> Then we will no longer be immature like children. We won't be tossed and blown about by every wind of new teaching. We will not be influenced when people try to trick us with lies so clever they sound like the truth. Instead, we will speak the truth in love, growing in every way more and more like Christ, who is the head of his body, the church. He makes the whole body fit together

perfectly. As each part does its own special work, it helps the other parts grow, so that the whole body is healthy and growing and full of love. (Ephesians 4:11–16)

How has God uniquely equipped you for building up the body of Christ?

How does your personal journey of renewal impact others around you (family, friends, coworkers, etc.)? How does it affect the church?

If every person in a church practiced the habit of learning and applying what Scripture says over applying man-made traditions, what do you think would change?

What could you change about your personal spiritual habits that would prevent you from being "tossed about" by every new idea that comes along?

We've explored renewal through the concepts represented by the words redeem, restart, repurpose, revive, rejoice, and repeat. Using the life of the apostle Paul and his letters written after his amazing transformation, we have an example and instructions for how to live. Let's close with the words of Paul himself:

> Get rid of all bitterness, rage, anger, harsh words, and slander, as well as all types of evil behavior. Instead, be kind to each other, tenderhearted, forgiving one another, just as God through Christ has forgiven you. (Ephesians 4:31–32)

That is what it means to be remade in the image of Jesus!

As you repeat and continue to pursue renewal, what excites you the most?

What are you most apprehensive about?

Who can you partner with to mutually encourage one another on your spiritual fitness plan?

Prayer Journal

I'M THANKFUL FOR:

_____

_____

_____

_____

_____

_____

I'M ASKING GOD FOR:

_____

_____

_____

_____

_____

_____

WORDS OF WORSHIP TO GOD:

_____

_____

_____

_____

_____

_____

APPLY

MICRO STUDY 1

Read 1 Peter 1:3–5.

Write out verse 4 here:

_____

_____

_____

_____

_____

_____

_____

> **Peter** (*Petros*, also called *Cephas*) was "an apostle of Jesus Christ and one of the three named pillars of the early church in Jerusalem." He was "the first Christian missionary to the Gentiles, a Christian missionary to the Jews, and a Christian martyr in Rome." Peter (Simon Peter) was one of Jesus's first disciples, the Twelve.[*]

The apostle Peter wrote this letter to encourage Christian friends who were experiencing suffering. You'll notice some of the same themes here that Paul included in his letters to Christians. Peter began with a reminder of the value of what they were suffering for.

What did Peter say about renewal?

---

* Jason Gish, "Peter the Apostle," in *The Lexham Bible Dictionary*, ed. John D. Barry et al. (Bellingham, WA: Lexham Press, 2016).

The Amplified Bible gives additional insight:

> Blessed [gratefully praised and adored] be the God and Father of our Lord Jesus Christ, who according to His abundant and boundless mercy has caused us to be

born again [that is, to be reborn from above—spiritually transformed, renewed, and set apart for His purpose] to an ever-living hope *and* confident assurance through the resurrection of Jesus Christ from the dead. (1 Peter 1:3 AMP)

Being reborn (something I will cover in depth in a later Bible study in the REMADE series) sounds like a restart, doesn't it? What was the priceless inheritance of which Peter spoke?

How often do you think the recipients re-read this letter for encouragement? Re-reading God's Scripture is our way of repeating the truth, a source of encouragement for whatever we face. Perhaps you read a Bible passage that you've heard many times, and suddenly God gives you new insights. Explain why the Bible isn't like a novel we read once and put on a shelf.

Peter said they lived with great expectation. Why?

What inspires you about what you studied today?

My prayer to God today is:

_____

_____

_____

_____

_____

_____

_____

_____

MICRO STUDY 2

Read 1 Peter 1:6–7.

Write out verse 6 here:

_____

_____

_____

_____

_____

_____

_____

Depending on the translation you use, verse 6 might talk about rejoicing, being glad, being very happy, or having tremendous joy. What is it that they had joy over? (Look back at yesterday's study if you need help.)

Would you say they were rejoicing over a place or a Person?

These verses remind me of a verse from Hebrews.

> We do this by keeping our eyes on Jesus, the champion who initiates and perfects our faith. Because of the joy awaiting him, he endured the cross, disregarding its shame. Now he is seated in the place of honor beside God's throne. (Hebrews 12:2)

Notice how Jesus kept his eyes on the joy ahead rather than the suffering he had to endure in the moment. How do these examples encourage you in what you're going through right now?

Some translations refer to the joy in verse 6 as an inexpressible joy. Why is it difficult to explain how you can have joy when you're suffering?

Our joy points beyond grief and the struggle. But notice how that suffering also *strengthens* the joy. It provides a testing process. Edmund P. Clowney explained it this way:

> The fires of affliction or persecution will not reduce our faith to ashes. *Fire* does not destroy gold: it only removes combustible impurities. Yet even gold will at last vanish with the whole of this created order. Faith is infinitely more precious and more enduring. Like a jeweller putting his most precious metal in the crucible, so God proves us in the furnace of trial and affliction. The genuineness of our faith shines from the fire to his praise.[*]

How has your faith been tested by what you have experienced in life?

How has that testing refined your faith?

---

[*] Edmund P. Clowney, *The Message of 1 Peter: The Way of the Cross, The Bible Speaks Today* (Leicester, England; Downers Grove, IL: InterVarsity Press, 1988), 52.

My prayer to God today is:

_____

_____

_____

_____

_____

_____

_____

_____

MICRO STUDY 3

Read 1 Peter 1:8–12.

Write out verse 8 here:

_____

_____

_____

_____

_____

_____

Notice how Peter brought up love here. Would you be willing to suffer for someone you didn't love?

How does loving Jesus make suffering for his sake sweeter?

What things in your life diminish your love, belief, and your joy in Christ?

Peter encouraged those who had faced suffering to look for the glory. Let's get a little context here about the author of the passage. Peter promised that he would never turn his back on Jesus. But in the moments when Jesus was being tortured and questioned before his death, Peter was out in the courtyard and swore to a bystander that he didn't know Jesus. I don't blame him. Do you? After the resurrection, Jesus gave Peter a chance to recommit his love to his Savior. Peter got a second chance.

Knowing that Jesus has mercy for even those who waver when trials are the worst, how does that encourage you?

How does knowing Peter's backstory make his letter even more encouraging?

In what situations do you doubt your faith or the certainty of your eternal future?

What assurance do you have from the Scripture you studied today?

My prayer to God today is:

_____

_____

_____

_____

_____

_____

_____

_____

MICRO STUDY 4

Read 1 Peter 1:13–21.

Write out verses 14–15 here:

_____

_____

_____

_____

_____

_____

_____

_____

_____

> Greek: hagios. adj. **holy, set apart, consecrated, dedicated, saints.** This refers to the quality of God who is transcendently distinctive, unique, majestic, perfect, and pure. When used about humans, it means being set apart for divine purposes.[*]

What comes to mind for you when you see Peter's instruction to the Christians to be holy?

* Hon-Lee Kwok, "Holiness," in *Lexham Theological Wordbook*, ed. Douglas Mangum et al., Lexham Bible Reference Series (Bellingham, WA: Lexham Press, 2014).

What is the difference between God's holiness and our holiness?

Does holiness sound impossible for you?

God has already made us holy, set apart, in Christ. He has saved us and called us his own. He urged us to be separate from what we used to be. Now he asks us to make choices that reflect who we *already are*. You already have your identity in Jesus. Now he's asking you to change your actions to align with that identity.

How does it change your perspective to think of yourself as *already* set apart when you are a believer versus striving to *become* set apart?

God doesn't expect perfection. But he does expect us to live based on the price that was already paid to save us from an empty life. Notice terms in this passage that have been part of our study over the last six weeks. Depending on your translation, you'll find the word *ransom* or *redeem* in verse 18.

How do you feel when you pause to think of how much Jesus loves you?

How does it feel to know your empty and guilty past cannot lock you up in shame or regret?

Knowing all of this, how would you define hope?

My prayer to God today is:

_____

_____

_____

_____

_____

_____

_____

MICRO STUDY 5

Read 1 Peter 1:22–25.

Write out verse 22 here:

_____

_____

_____

_____

_____

_____

_____

_____

_____

What did Peter say should be the result of stepping into our identity in Jesus Christ (verse 22)?

What do you think it means to love someone deeply?

Explain why this is different from love that comes and goes based on conditions.

Again, Peter talked about being born again. Some Christians toss this term around like a title. That isn't what it is. Remember what you learned this week about renewal. It's a chance to start over with a brand-new life. Paul experienced it dramatically. Peter experienced it after he crumbled under pressure and then Jesus gave him another chance.

Peter quoted Isaiah 40:6–8 here in these verses. This new life we have through faith in Jesus isn't like grass or even a perennial flower that grows up, blooms for a season, and withers at the first hard frost. And it isn't like human procreation, which produces temporary bodies. We have an everlasting relationship with Jesus in God's family.

What has God been challenging you to renew during these weeks of study?

Some translations refer to a "living hope" in 1 Peter 1:3 where Peter referenced being born again. Here in verse 23, Peter wrote about God's living Word. God has planted a seed in you that will never die.

Although our time on earth is short, our lives go on for eternity. How is your faith renewed today because of that truth?

What will you do to nurture that seed and grow spiritually?

Pray, asking God to reveal where he wants to work on you. Then finish this sentence: Because I am renewed in Jesus Christ, my next growth step is _____.

My prayer to God today is:

_____

_____

_____

_____

_____

_____

_____

_____

Hope in Action

THERE ARE MANY WAYS TO EXPRESS WORSHIP inside and outside of church. As you complete this study on being renewed, find a creative way to express your gratitude and thanks to God for what he has done in you. Try worshiping through writing a poem or a song, making a painting or a sculpture, planting a garden, drawing a picture, making a collage, painting a mural, making a quilt—anything that enriches your creative expression to God.

Invite friends to work on a project together and make it a time of celebration and worship.

Anything that reminds you of God's renewing grace and mercy can be a memorial. When Joshua and the Israelites crossed miraculously into the promised land over the Jordan River—God stopped the flooded river for them to cross—they set up a pile of twelve stones to serve as a memorial of what God had done (Joshua 4:2–8).

Notes

Notes

Notes

Benediction

IT'S BEEN A JOY TO SPEND THESE weeks with you! As we close out this study, I'll leave you with a blessing from the apostle Paul's words.

> Now may our Lord Jesus Christ himself and God our Father, who loved us and by his grace gave us eternal comfort and a wonderful hope, comfort you and strengthen you in every good thing you do and say. (2 Thessalonians 2:16–17)

Michelle

LOOK FOR OTHER BOOKS IN THE REMADE SERIES:

Acknowledgments

MY STORY OF RENEWAL DIDN'T HAPPEN IN a vacuum. There are so many people to thank.

It begins with Jesus, and I thank him for his unimaginable grace and love as I bumble my way through being human and trying to live by his pattern. Without him, none of what I write would have meaning. He is my story and security.

God put a fun-loving and kind teenage boy in my path in 1985, and it's been a journey! I'm glad I said yes to that awkward request for a first date. Phil, you've been with me through every peak and valley—from "I think I want to be a writer" to writing articles, to my first published book, to now. I'm so grateful for a husband who believes in my calling and urges me to press on, even if I regularly leave you a pile of dishes to clean up or you come home after work to nothing simmering on the stove. You listen to all sorts of brainstorming nonsense that flows from my mouth when you want to kick back and watch TV. You're the best of the nice guys.

Mom and Dad, you modeled the foundation of a Christian home from the moment I was born. That heritage ripples to several generations now.

My boys and daughters-in-love: Dallas and Austin, and Amy and Alyssa, you are so wonderful about respecting boundaries when I need to be in my office. Thank you all for taking my work seriously and honoring what God has called me to do.

Lin Johnson, Jane Rubietta, and the Write-to-Publish Conference staff over the years, you gave me a foundation of tools and encouragement and opened doors for a freelance career to grow.

Robyn Mulder, I'm so glad we met. Great editors are priceless. Thank you for your keen eye for mistakes. Jill Stanish, thank you for doing a final sweep in every corner!

Kathy Carlton Willis, when our paths first crossed, I had no idea they would someday run parallel as cohorts in the writing and publishing business. I appreciate the industry chats, but even more, your friendship. Thank you for being a safe confidant as I wrestle through God's re-purposing and renewing. It isn't as lonely when someone has your back!

Soul Sisters: Barb, Terri, Vergene, Maureen, and Joyce. Thank you for being ready to pray at all times and letting me blubber whenever needed.

Reader, this is for you. Thank you for purchasing this book and putting it to use. I hunkered down in a cabin to write a lot of this study, and I pictured you sitting across the table from me—although I left you hardly any room with the Bibles, notebook, commentaries, chocolate treats, and iced latte there. When I wrapped myself in a blanket and watched the sunrise, I asked God to make himself known to you in the same way and with the same sense of peace as you study his Word.

May the LORD bless you
and protect you.
May the LORD smile on you
and be gracious to you.
May the LORD show you his favor
and give you his peace.

—Numbers 6:24–26

About the Author

MICHELLE RAYBURN DELIGHTS IN REPURPOSED JUNK, GREAT books, dark chocolate, and iced coffee—and summer Sunday afternoons in the hammock with the latter three. As a writer and podcast host, she helps others discover the joy of finding hope in the trashy stuff of life. The *Life Repurposed* podcast (awarded 2020 Spark Outstanding Podcast Host, Female) features guest stories of renewed faith.

Among Michelle's books are *Classic Marriage* (winner of a Golden Scroll Award, Christian Market Book Award, and finalist in Next Gen Indie Book Awards), *The Repurposed and Upcycled Life* (Write-to-Publish Writer of the Year award), and *Life, Repurposed*, which features the amazing stories of 34 women (Golden Scroll Award honorable mention).

Michelle has a master's in ministry leadership with a pastoral counseling emphasis. She enjoys speaking for women's events where she can blend Bible teaching with humor and wisdom from life's imperfect moments.

She and her high school sweetheart, Phil, have been fine-tuning their classic marriage for more than three decades. They've raised two boys, and the family tree has branched to include two daughters-in-law and three grandchildren (and counting). They make their home in the Northwoods of Wisconsin in a century-old former church and parsonage.

www.michellerayburn.com

Anyone who belongs to Christ has become a *new person*. The old life is gone; a *new life* has begun!

2 Cor. 5:17

A free printable 8x10 art image inspired by this book series is waiting for you at

WWW.MICHELLERAYBURN.COM/REMADE

If you've enjoyed this book, please write a review on your favorite bookstore platform and help spread the word about the series. Thank you!

Made in United States
Troutdale, OR
01/02/2025